Jackrabbit Tales

Jackrabbit Tales

Doug & Shirley,

Go Jacks!

by V.J. Smith

Copyright © 2009
by V.J. Smith

ALL RIGHTS RESERVED

This work may not be used in any form, or reproduced by any means, in whole or in part, without written permission from the publisher.

ISBN: 978-1-57579-399-3

Library of Congress Control Number: 2009924380

Printed in the United States of America

PINE HILL PRESS
4000 West 57th Street
Sioux Falls, SD 57106

To Earl Martell, my junior high science teacher in Eureka, South Dakota. When I was in the seventh grade he took me to a science fair at South Dakota State University. It was love at first sight.

He was the best teacher I ever had.

About the Author

V.J. Smith served as the director of the South Dakota State University Alumni Association for ten years. Prior to that, he was an assistant to the athletic director for six years. A native of Eureka, South Dakota, he graduated from SDSU in 1978. Now a full-time professional speaker and published author, Smith travels throughout the United States sharing encouragement and gratitude.

V.J. Smith is the author of "Jackrabbit Tales" and "The Richest Man in Town."

Check out his website: www.lifesgreatmoments.com

CONTENTS

The Lady From Chicago 1
Carpe Diem 7
Fire! 13
Run, Josh, Run 17
The Major 21
The Howlers 27
That Great Big Beautiful Band 33
Liberation Day 41
Charlie's Angel 49
Hurling Critters And Stuff 55
Sentimental Journey 59
Remembering Warren 63
Steel Mallets 67
Top 'Rabbits 73
My Original Dr. Phil 79
The Hat Lady 83
A Giant Of A Man 87
Promotions Gone Bad 95
The Year That Wasn't 103
Making A Difference 109
A Capital Experience 115
The Tidy Dean 119
Hall Of Famer 121
Coming Of Age 125
Meeting Royalty 129
A Long Way From Home 135

An Observation

A few years ago, after speaking to an assembly of teachers, the superintendent of schools approached the microphone and said, "*I don't know who* would want to buy his book, but if you are interested you can purchase one after we are done here."

There was a moment of awkward silence, enough time for the audience to absorb the comment, and soon the low rumble of chuckles turned into all-out laughter. The superintendent grew red-faced. He realized the way he said it wasn't what he meant.

I thought it was funny. And, I still do.

It's an odd feeling that people would actually pay for something I've written. To be honest, I think Mrs. Kitzler, my high school English teacher, would feel the same way.

You need to know that I've never considered myself a real author. That would be an insult to the many gifted wordsmiths of the world who make writing an art form. All I do is share stories about what I know.

Besides, I can't help but think of something an old friend told me not too long ago. His name is Wayne and he's been a carpenter for more than thirty years. We've known each other since we were five years old. Wayne said, "Schmitty, you're not very bright but you try to pay attention. I'm not very bright but I can lift heavy objects. We both need to be able to do something."

Mind you, I was an average student. I was lucky to have Dr. Robert Burns and Dr. John Miller as my advisors while I attended South Dakota State University. Both were brilliant professors with a deep appreciation for history. They instilled in me the need to remember the past.

I graduated from SDSU in 1978 with degrees in political science and history. My working career at the university included a two-year stint in the Admission's Office (1979-1981), Assistant to the Athletic Director (1990-1996), and Director of the Alumni Association (1996-2006). There is an indescribable energy level on a college campus that can't be duplicated anywhere else. It was an honor to work at my alma mater.

For selfish reasons, I wanted to record some memories about people and events that shaped my experience at SDSU. I didn't want them to get lost with the passage of time.

I want to thank Sherry Fuller Bordewyk for editing this book. Her talents made a huge difference in this project. Plus, I love her compassionate heart.

You will notice the chapters aren't very long. I hope you find a chapter or two you enjoy.

It's a great day to be a Jackrabbit!

The Lady from Chicago

"Sir, I have two questions for you," said the soft voice on the other end of the phone line on a September day in 1992.

"First, do you have a track program at South Dakota State University?" I replied that we did. "Second, do you give scholarships to those kids?"

"Yes," I said.

"Congratulations, I'm going to send you forty-thousand dollars."

And that's how a ten-year affair with Mildred White started. Simple, to the point, and filled with surprises.

Mildred lived in Wilmette, Illinois, a suburb north of Chicago. She was eighty years old and fully engaged. Roger, her late husband, had graduated from Washington High School in Sioux Falls in 1929. Mildred followed a year later. In the fall of 1929, Roger, a track star in high school, enrolled at State but was forced to quit by year's end. America was on the cusp of the Great Depression.

Roger and Mildred, high school sweethearts, married shortly after she graduated. He began work with Montgomery Ward in Sioux City. Eventually, he became the company's top salesman in the furniture division. One day he came home and said to Mildred, "Honey, we could make a lot more money if we made the furniture and sold it for ourselves. How about we open our own furniture company?"

They did and they became millionaires. Well, millionaires die, too. Unfortunately, Roger died in 1972 at age 62 due to a brain aneurysm. Twenty years later Mildred decided to start a scholarship in Roger's name on our campus.

For the next ten years, I talked to Mildred about once a week. I visited her two to three times a year at her home in Wilmette. Twice I flew to Chicago, rented a car, picked her up at her home, and drove her all the way back to South Dakota. You get to know a lot about a person spending eleven hours in the car together.

On our first trip back to South Dakota, we were driving through Milwaukee, Wisconsin, and I asked her, "Are you hungry?" She replied, "Yes. Just pick a place. I don't really care." So, I stopped at a Hardee's restaurant. When we walked inside, she said, "This must be some kind of burger joint." When she asked for a Cobb salad with oil and vinegar, I knew she was of limited information regarding fast food operations.

I always hated it when she saw a dead animal on the road. She was a great animal lover and it pained her to see roadkill. After driving past a dead creature, we would spend the next five minutes talking about what the critter may have eaten for its last meal. So, whenever I saw a dead deer or raccoon in the distance, I would point out something on the opposite side of the road, hoping to deflect her attention.

Speaking of animals, she fed a half dozen stray, wild cats that came to her door every day. One evening, after

Mildred and I had gone out to eat at a local restaurant, we arrived back at her home and spotted three cats sitting on her door stoop. She said, "Oh, look at my kitties!" When I got of the car and approached them, they hissed at me.

On many occasions Mildred would say to me, "We must be doing something bad to the environment. I just don't see as many birds as I used to."

I think the hissing cats ate them.

Another thing I learned about Mildred was that she was no pushover. She held strong opinions on a variety of things. One was about her former son-in-law. "I knew it wouldn't last. The first time I saw him he was wearing a blue suit and had on brown shoes. Who wears brown shoes with a blue suit?"

I never went to see her wearing brown shoes with a blue suit.

By the way, the only time I ever asked Mildred for money was when the women's basketball locker room was being renovated. She gave us $3,500. Through our conversations it became apparent that she disdained organizations that were constantly asking for money. She preferred to do things on her own, without being pushed.

That is how the South Dakota Art Museum received $350,000 from her. On one of her trips to SDSU, I took her there to see the artwork. She started receiving the museum's newsletter and noticed an article about the expansion project. Mildred called me and said, "How much do they need to finish that deal?"

In time, Mildred created five scholarships in the athletic department. The last one was named for her beloved dachshund, Dacotah. That's right, there is a scholarship in the SDSU athletic department named for a wiener dog. Mildred loved that dog and lamented about what would happen when it died. She would tell me, "When the dog dies, I'm going, too."

Dacotah died in January 2002. Mildred called me and said, "It cost me $500 to have her cremated. I don't care. Make sure when they bury me, they bury the dog's ashes with me."

Two months later, Mildred was dead.

I still remember standing over Mildred's casket – her wearing a beautiful dress – and noticing the box containing Dacotah's ashes underneath her hands. True to that dog until the end.

True to us, too. A month after returning from her funeral, the administrator of her estate contacted us to say that Mildred left SDSU almost three million dollars. She specified that it go to the scholarship program.

A part of Mildred's largesse went to Northwestern University. She was a great benefactor to that school, too. Every year, Northwestern University sponsors the Mildred and Roger White Basketball Tournament, featuring top-notch women's college basketball teams. Mildred loved women's basketball.

To be honest, Northwestern University wasn't thrilled with the attention we gave to Mildred. They viewed us as a threat. I always believed if Mildred had stopped giving us gifts after the initial $40,000, we still owed her our respect, appreciation and attention. It was the proper thing to do.

Besides, Mildred was in control and she knew exactly what was going on. That was made crystal clear to me in March 1996.

Mildred called me and asked if I would take her to an event at a swanky hotel in Evanston, Illinois. Northwestern University's football coach, Gary Barnett, was going to receive an award for being named the top college coach in the country. His team had made it to the Rose Bowl the previous New Year's Day. I was thrilled to go.

We arrived an hour before the start of the social. Like most people of her generation, Mildred always wanted to be early. As we were standing and waiting in the hotel lobby, a man approached Mildred. He was Rick Taylor, the athletic director at Northwestern University.

He grabbed Mildred's hands, leaned forward and kissed her on the cheek. After a few moments, Mildred said, "Rick, I want to introduce you to V.J. Smith."

Taylor shook my hand and said, "Hello, B.J." Mildred caught the mistake and said, "His name is *V.*J. He's from South Dakota State University." She paused for a moment and added, "Rick, meet your competition." She howled at her remark.

I miss her.

Carpe Diem
[Sieze the Day]

Lou Holtz was partly responsible for the SDSU history book "The College on the Hill." Yes, *that* Lou Holtz – the former head football coach at Notre Dame and now a television sports analyst.

This is going to require a bit of an explanation so let me take a running start at it.

Back in 1989, when I lived in Kansas City, I watched a video of Holtz giving a speech. He had spoken of the importance of setting goals.

Holtz said that in 1967 the entire football staff at the University of South Carolina was fired. Since he was an assistant coach he got the boot, too. He was thirty years old, his wife was pregnant with their third child, his car needed repairs and he needed a job.

His wife, being the supportive sort, gave him a book on setting goals. The book instructed the reader to take a paper and pencil and write down everything they dreamed about doing in life. Lou started writing. He wrote down 107 goals. The goals included skydiving, having dinner at the White House, being on "The Tonight Show with Johnny Carson," and becoming the head football coach at Notre Dame. Pretty heady stuff for a guy who just got canned at South Carolina.

Lou was proud of his list and showed it to his wife. After going through all 107 goals she said, "Lou, you got a pencil?" He gave one to her. She wrote: "#108 – get a job."

Holtz has achieved almost one hundred of the goals he set in 1967. In fact, when he took the head football job at the University of Minnesota in 1984, he had it written into his contract that he could break that agreement if he was ever offered the job at Notre Dame. After two successful seasons with the Gophers, he left for the Golden Dome in South Bend, Indiana.

They still hate him in Minnesota for that.

For six years I thought about Lou Holtz and writing a list of goals. Finally, on my 40th birthday I got busy. Seriously, I sat down at my computer that night and typed in bold letters: "Goals for My Lifetime." I listed fifty-seven things.

The third goal I typed was to write a book. I didn't have a clue what it would be about. Lots of people entertain thoughts on writing a book. Some even get it done and their garages or basements are now filled with dusty boxes of unsold books. It's the risk you take.

Six years after writing that goal, in September 2001, I got an idea. It came to me while signing sympathy cards to families of recently deceased alumni. Each time a graduate died a part of SDSU history was lost, too.

A light went on in my head. We needed to record the personal history of the campus. No more lost stories – it was time to start writing. Besides, stories about people are far more interesting than stories about buildings.

Shortly after making the decision to do the book, I saw Amy Dunkle in the post office. She had recently left her position at *The Brookings Register* and I knew she was a talented writer. So I asked her if she wanted a job.

I did much of the research and figured out the chapters, and Amy did the writing. Two years later, in October 2003, "The College on the Hill" arrived.

So, did I achieve my goal? No, I did not write the book. Amy did.

As I reflect on it, my greatest satisfaction was recording the eyewitness accounts of important moments in the history of the university. Many of the people who were interviewed for the book have since died. Sadly, we were never able to interview former president Hilton Briggs as he was killed in a car accident a few months after we started the project.

Over time, I've received criticism that we failed to include certain people or events. I suppose it goes with the territory.

One evening I was eating at a local restaurant and was approached by a well-known and respected man in the community. He asked why there wasn't a chapter on former Senator Tom Daschle. I told him that the book was about the people, times and events shaping the life of the university. Certainly if a book is ever written about the most notable graduates of SDSU, Tom Daschle would be the subject of one chapter.

The man said, "He was student body president!" I said he wasn't. He shook his head, said I was wrong and walked away. Well, I'm wrong on a lot of things but I'm not on that one.

Dwight Eisenhower's visit to the campus on October 4, 1952, evoked a myth that does not die. Eisenhower was campaigning for president and spoke to 12,000 people assembled at the Coolidge Sylvan Theatre. He jumped into the Bummobile, the iconic symbol of Hobo Day that was parked nearby, and had his picture taken. That's all he did.

Years later, there are many people who swear they saw him riding in the Bummobile in the Hobo Day parade. I know there are a lot of people who claim to see many things during the Hobo Day parade, but Eisenhower wasn't one of them. Hobo Day was still two weeks away.

Sid Bostic's 40-foot desperation shot to win the 1963 national basketball tournament is a source for another mystery. More than one team member claims to have passed the basketball to Bostic before his famous toss. It's hard to imagine with that many people watching the play develop that there could be confusion. In the mayhem of the moment, details were lost. I'm sorry if we got that one wrong.

Mistakes and omissions aside, it is difficult to compress the history of SDSU into a mere six hundred pages. We tried the best we could.

And, as I reflect on all of this, the best thing I received from that project was a major dose of reality. I thought a lot about my own mortality.

Day after day as I sifted through the withered and yellowing pages of old newspapers and yearbooks, I saw the smiling faces of countless young people staring back at me. Armed with youthful optimism and big dreams, they were eager to conquer a new world. Nothing could stop them – nothing.

But, most of them are gone now. One day, I'll be gone, too.

An image I could never shed during the entire time I spent researching the book came courtesy of the movie "Dead Poets Society." The 1989 film starred Robin Williams as an English teacher at a conservative all-male prep school.

There's a poignant moment when he shepherds his students into a hallway filled with dozens of old photographs. The photos were of young men who had attended the school many years before.

The teacher urges the students to get close to the pictures and look into the faces of the past. Then he says, "They're not that different from you, are they? Same haircuts. Full of hormones, just like you. Invincible, just like you feel. The world is their oyster. They believe they're destined for great things, just like many of you. Their eyes are full of hope, just like you. Did they wait until it was too late to make their lives even one iota of what they were capable? Because you see gentlemen, these boys are now fertilizing daffodils. But, if you listen real close, you can hear them whisper their legacy to you. Go on, lean in."

The students inch forward. Then, in a whispered tone and pretending to be the voice of the young men pictured, the teacher softly cries out, "Carpe." The teacher pauses and in his normal voice asks, "Hear it?"

After a brief moment, he again begins to whisper as if he is a voice from the past, "Carpe...carpe diem. Seize the day boys, make your lives extraordinary."

FIRE!

I'm not sure how many miles I drove as alumni director, but it seemed like I was in the car a lot. Most times, it was just endless roads and nothing much happened.

In May 2002, coming back from an alumni event in the Black Hills, I saw something that continues to make me chuckle to this day. I was heading east on Interstate 90 and pulled off at the rest area just outside Wasta, South Dakota. It was late morning and I needed to take a quick nap.

I maneuvered my car under the shade of a tree and opened my windows. The cool air washed over me and I soon found myself at the brink of blissful sleep. Just then I caught a whiff of smoke. I jumped up, looked out the windshield and checked the hood of my car – nothing. I scanned the interior of my car and didn't notice anything wrong, so I laid back and shut my eyes.

Two seconds later a woman yelled, "Well, somebody ought to call the Wasta fire department!"

That had my attention. So, I sat up again and looked to my left. Fifty feet away were two guys hovering over a brand new black Ford Bronco. The vehicle was connected to a large, white RV by a tow bar. Flames were shooting out from underneath the hood of the Bronco.

The two guys couldn't open up the hood because of the intense heat. One of them held a fire extinguisher in front of the windshield, trying to shoot white powder through the narrow crack between the glass and the hood, down into the engine. It didn't work.

The fire got hotter and the guys realized the RV could catch on fire, too. One of them jumped into the driver's seat of the RV and quickly drove it over to a watering station located at the same rest stop. Someone grabbed a hose, which wasn't much bigger than a typical garden hose, and started spraying the front of the Bronco.

While one guy held the hose, trying to keep the flames at bay, the other guy heroically disconnected the tow bar that tied the two vehicles together. That accomplished, the RV moved one hundred feet forward, leaving the Bronco by itself.

In the distance I could hear the wail of a siren. "Good," I thought, "a fire truck." In the meantime, I watched a brand new vehicle being swallowed by a growing fire. Windows were popping, tires were exploding, and the stench of thick black smoke filled the air.

The fire truck pulled up beside the burning vehicle. Two firemen, decked out in slick firemen gear and wearing helmets, jumped from their truck and started grabbing hoses. They began to spray a white foam on the once proud Bronco. I noticed a sign on the door of the truck: Wall Fire Department. The town was ten miles down the road.

Ten minutes later, another vehicle arrived. It was an old truck with a small flatbed in the back. Sitting on the flatbed was a barrel filled with water. Two guys, both wearing white T-shirts and blue jeans, exited the vehicle and one of them grabbed a hose and started shooting a small stream of water at the skeletal remains of the Bronco. While one guy sprayed, the other guy smoked a cigarette. It was Wasta's Fire Department.

On that day I learned two lessons. First, if you are going to tow a vehicle with an RV, make sure the transmission is in neutral. The owner of the Bronco left the gear in the drive mode, thus overheating the engine. Second, if you are going to have a fire, try to have it in Wall and not in Wasta.

Run, Josh, Run

Josh Ranek was the most exciting football player I ever saw wearing the yellow and blue colors of South Dakota State University. Inside his five-foot, nine-inch muscular frame beat the heart of a lion.

In the mid-'90s, while watching high school football highlights on television on Friday nights, the sports anchors would focus on a powerful running back from Tyndall, South Dakota – Josh Ranek. He wasn't very big. But he always seemed to be in the end zone.

After high school football season, Josh turned his attention to wrestling. He was a champion in that sport, too.

So, I was familiar with his name when he came to SDSU. Of course, high school success oftentimes does not translate into success at the collegiate level.

During fall football camp in 1996, I heard several remarks from coaches who used the words "punishing" and "exciting" when they described Josh's running abilities. Honestly, in my six years in the athletic department, there were only a handful of recruited athletes who made the coaches giddy. Josh was one of them.

As he redshirted in 1996, the Jackrabbit faithful had to wait until September 1997 for his debut. It would be on the campus of the University of California-Davis. Or, as the folks out there like to be called, UC-Davis.

I was sitting on the bleachers, taking in a little California sun, when the Jackrabbit football team ran onto the field to do pre-game drills. A group of five guys sat behind me – all UC-Davis fans. There was a lot of discussion and laughter. Then, they placed their bets.

They had this game where they surveyed and evaluated players of the opposing team during the warm-ups. Then, they would wager on which player they thought would be the last one to see playing time. Mostly they were looking for size.

One of the guys bet on Josh, or against Josh, however you want to look at it. He was shocked when Josh took the field early. "Why the hell is he in there?" he said to his friends. By the end of the game, even that guy was cheering for Josh.

He ran for 98 yards. It was the way he ran that excited the fans. He didn't dance behind some big lineman, waiting for a hole to open up. Instead, he took the ball from the quarterback and sprinted, full bore, into the line of scrimmage. If he broke free of the line and a defensive back was waiting for him, Josh simply lowered his helmet and punished the guy for being in his way.

By the time Josh ended his college career in 2001, he had put the hurt on a lot of defensive players. Then, he played football in the Canadian Football League. In Ottawa, playing for the Renegades, his teammates dubbed him "The Little Ball of Hate." It was the physical toll he extracted on the opponents that earned him the nickname.

To that end, Josh was a bit of an enigma. Off the field, he was a quiet, soft-spoken young man. And, he was always polite.

That, too, is why I liked him so much. So often – too often – athletes will make some play on the court or field and will beat their breasts as if they conquered the world.

Not Josh. After he scored a touchdown, he simply handed the football to a referee. I remember a fan asking John Stiegelmeier, the head coach football coach, why Josh wasn't demonstrative – doing a little dance or spiking the ball – after scoring a touchdown. He said, "If he did, he would know I would talk to him. But, before I got to him, his dad would already be talking to him."

I loved that answer.

Josh got into the end zone a lot. He holds North Central Conference records for touchdowns and rushing yardage. Heck, he owns a lot of records. Josh finished his career running for 6,794 yards.

To put this into perspective, he ran with a football in his hands for almost four miles. All the while, eleven guys on the other side of the line were trying to tear his head off.

As the North Central Conference no longer exists, his records will never be broken.

Before sitting down to write this chapter, I sent Coach Stiegelmeier a note and asked him if there was a video featuring highlights of Josh's career. I remembered the 1999 Hobo Day football game against the University of North Dakota where he caught a screen pass and broke six tackles to score a touchdown. Then, there was the last second two-point conversion against Augustana in 2000, when everyone in Howard Wood Stadium, including the Vikings, knew he was going to get the ball. It didn't matter. Josh scored and the Jacks won, 25-24, after being down 24-0 at halftime. I wanted to relive those great highlights.

Stiegelmeier wrote back, "His career was a highlight."

That said it all.

THE MAJOR

This is a story I can't shake.

In the fall of 1912, Cleve Abbott arrived on the South Dakota State campus. He wasn't your typical freshman student. Abbott, who was born in Yankton and raised in Watertown, South Dakota, was a man of color.

Can you imagine how much courage it took to come to a lily-white college in 1912?

When he arrived, he was undecided about a major. He was assigned to the dairy building to pay for his room and board. At registration, a faculty adviser asked him about his field of study. Abbott, embarrassed by not having a major in mind, yet remembering his new work assignment, simply answered, "dairying."

The irony is that he was a city kid. He had never worked on a farm before. Yet, four years later, he would graduate with a degree in dairy husbandry.

Abbott was a good student and a gifted athlete. In time, he earned fourteen varsity letters participating in football, basketball, baseball and track. In 1968, he became the second person inducted into the Jackrabbit Athletic Hall of Fame. That's remarkable considering he had graduated fifty-two years before. Many of the people who witnessed his exploits were gone – yet, his legend lived on.

But, let's go back to the spring of 1913.

A national education conference was held in New York City. The president of South Dakota State, Ellwood Perisho attended the event. So did Booker T. Washington, the president of Tuskegee Institute and the leading African-American spokesman in the country.

Yes, *that* Booker T. Washington.

The two presidents met on the train when they were leaving the conference. Washington wanted to start a sports program at Tuskegee to attract and retain greater numbers of young people. He asked Perisho if he had any young men who might qualify as a sports director.

Perisho told him about Abbott, but said he was only a freshman and needed to prove himself. Washington told Perisho, "You go back and tell this young man, if he will be a good boy and study hard, he can be my sports director when he graduates from college."

When Perisho returned to South Dakota, he shared the good news with Abbott. Sadly, Booker T. Washington died in November 1915. Abbott thought his job was gone, too.

In March 1916, three months before Abbott graduated, a surprise letter arrived from Tuskegee. Washington's secretary had been going through some files and found a memo of agreement for Abbott's employment. She sent a contract and offered him a job.

It wasn't for the sports director position. Instead, it was to take care of the dairy cows. But, he was prepared.

For more than a year, he was responsible for one hundred fifty Jersey cows, directed the cowhands, taught students on the dairy business and did some assistant coaching. Then, World War I came calling.

He saw the hell of war from the trenches in France. Writing to his father, Abbott reflected on the Battle of the Argonne Forest, the last great conflict of the war. He said, "It was an American victory and colored Americans helped make it so."

After the war, Abbott joined the faculty of Kansas Vocational School in Topeka, Kansas, where he coached and was commandant of cadets.

In 1923, Abbott returned to Tuskegee as the school's athletic director and head football coach – positions he held until 1955. During the next thirty-two seasons, his football teams had a record of 203 wins, 95 losses and 15 ties. He is the most successful football coach in the history of Tuskegee.

Students referred to him as "Major." Not coach. Not mister. It was a salutation of respect.

By the way, the football field at Tuskegee is now named Cleve L. Abbott Memorial Alumni Stadium. Not bad for a guy from the Dakota prairie.

But, it gets better.

He was a pioneer in women's track. For a period of four decades, he is said to have developed the program that opened track and field to women in the United States. Abbott was inducted into the USA Track & Field Hall of Fame in 1996.

Six of his athletes qualified for the Olympics. Alice Coachman won the high jump in 1948 at the London Games. She was the first black woman ever to win a gold medal. More than sixty-five thousand spectators at Wembley Stadium witnessed King George VI of England place the coveted medal around her neck.

I had the privilege of speaking to Ms. Coachman on the phone. She told me she was seventeen years old when Abbott showed up at her home in Albany, Georgia. He wanted her to come to Tuskegee but her father did not want her to go. She said, "I told my mom and dad that I was tired of picking cotton." That's exactly what she told me.

When I asked her what Abbott meant to her, she said, "At college, he was my mother, father, coach, doctor and banker. He was my everything."

Sixty years had passed since her moment of Olympic glory, yet it was all still fresh in her mind. The day before the high jump event, she received a telegram from Abbott, who wasn't able to accompany her to London. Coachman said the wire stated, "The higher you go, remember your takeoff."

Her former coach was reminding her to focus on the spot on the ground that she needed to hit before jumping. She said, "I won the gold medal because I remembered what the Major told me." Her leap of five-feet, six-and-a-fourth-inches was a new world record.

Basketball is a sport she continues to follow to this day. She said she was great at getting rebounds. "I could grab that ball out of the air, pass it to a teammate and they would go down and score before I hit the ground," she told me.

As I researched Abbott's life, I stumbled across something that made me giddy. He was partly responsible for the marriage of Evelyn Lawler and William Lewis. Abbott recruited Lawler for the track team and sought Lewis' services for the football team. They met at the Tuskegee campus, eventually wed, and produced four children – three boys and a girl.

In honor of their coach, they named a son Cleveland Abbott Lewis. He became a professional soccer player. Another son they named Carl.

Yes, *that* Carl Lewis – the most decorated track athlete in the history of the United States of America.

I got so excited I called the alumni director at Tuskegee to see if we could contact William and Evelyn Lewis. The director told me that Mr. Lewis was deceased and Mrs. Lewis lived in Houston, Texas. With a little coaxing, he gave me her address but added, "Don't make a pest of yourself."

A few days later, I sent a letter to Mrs. Lewis and explained our connection to Abbott. She called one week later, thrilled to be able to share stories about her former coach. During the course of the conversation, she said, "If there had never been a Major Abbott, there never would have been a Carl Lewis."

Just writing that sends chills down my spine.

Mixed in with all my favorite Abbott stories was a special moment born on a beautiful June day in 2002. A mother and son stopped by the alumni office. She was almost ninety years old and he was in his late 50s. The son explained to me that when his mother was five years old, her mother – his grandmother – cooked meals for college students who ate on campus.

Because it was such a gorgeous day, I suggested we sit outside. I grabbed some folding chairs and set them on the grass facing the Campus Green. Then, I went back inside the building and grabbed the 1916 yearbook, thinking she might remember some of the faces and places from that era.

After a few minutes of paging through the yearbook, the woman shrieked, "There he is!" It was a picture of Cleve Abbott. She took her hand and touched Abbott's face. "He was the first black man I ever saw," she said in a reflective voice. "I remember after shaking his hand, I quickly put mine behind my back. I'm embarrassed to say this, but when he walked away I looked at my hand thinking there would be some black on it. I didn't know."

The old woman sat in silence and just stared at the picture. I didn't want to interrupt her voyage back in time so I just sat and looked at her. Then she said, "He called me 'princess.' All my life I've tried to treat all people, but especially black people, the same way he treated me."

Cleve Abbott died in April 1955. Appropriately, he is buried near Booker T. Washington on the Tuskegee campus.

THE HOWLERS

A few years ago, bored on a Sunday afternoon, I was channel surfing my television set and came across a South Dakota Public Broadcasting show emanating from the University of South Dakota.

The late, great conservative writer and commentator William F. Buckley was the featured speaker. In his opening comments, Buckley said his friend, USD alumnus Tom Brokaw, had encouraged him to speak slowly "...so that the graduates of South Dakota State College of Agricultural and Mechanic Arts can understand what I am saying."

Red meat had been thrown to the Coyote faithful. They howled and clapped their approval. Laughter filled the hall.

I bristled.

A couple years later, famed CBS News reporter Bob Schieffer received an award at USD. In his remarks, Schieffer said he had attended Texas Christian University, home of the Horned Frogs. He said there were a lot of silly athletic mascots. But, Schieffer said, "I'd rather be a Horned Frog than a Jackrabbit."

It was more red meat for coyotes.

Why do they do that? I've been to hundreds of SDSU functions and I don't remember a single time when a speaker, on their own accord or encouraged by their hosts, took a swipe at USD.

I suppose you can dismiss it as innocent fun. It's always more fun to have someone else be the butt of jokes. For me, it's been a pattern I've witnessed my entire adult life. Disguised as good college humor, there has been a litany of putdowns, cheap shots and wisecracks often intended to question the intellect or background of SDSU students and alumni. Frankly, I think it is elitist and pervasive.

By the way, in October 2008, Brokaw spoke at the annual meeting of the Sioux Falls Chamber of Commerce. In his remarks, he praised his alma mater for its campaign to achieve excellence. He said that SDSU was pursuing excellence, too, and is now offering a doctorate degree in sheep shearing.

Good old Tom, stuck in 1962.

In the summer of 2005, a joint SDSU and USD alumni gathering was held in Kennebunk, Maine. Each graduate was asked to give a self-introduction and, perhaps, offer a few comments. A young alumna from USD began her remarks by saying she would use simple English so that the SDSU graduates in attendance could understand her.

The pattern starts early.

A USD student, writing in his student newspaper, summed up the attitude of generations of USD students when he wrote, "Questioning the intelligence of a person from South Dakota State is not only accepted, it is mandatory."

I'm not making this stuff up. And, please don't tell me that I need to lighten up or grow thick skin.

For years, USD officials have worked overtime to manufacture spin on how the Vermillion campus has cornered the market on the smartest students in the region. It's not true.

The featured story in the *Argus Leader* on Sunday, December 8, 2002, is a great example of what I'm writing about. The article said, in effect, that SDSU was placing its emphasis on moving to Division I athletics, while USD was concentrating on academics. Each school, according to the writer, had picked different paths to prestige.

USD's well-scripted propaganda machine prompted the reporter to write, "The school's president, Jim Abbott, said USD will center its resources on academics and might raise admission standards as part of what its marketers call a move to become an 'Ivy of the Plains.'"

A USD coach was quoted in the same article as saying that a move to Division I would overemphasize sports and amounted to "a case of the tail wagging the dog."

With USD's recent move to Division I, we all know what happened to *that* dog. It didn't hunt. But then, I digress.

The article left the reader with the impression that SDSU was choosing athletics over academics. And, it became fodder for a lot of coffee shop talk throughout the state. How could SDSU pick sports over a quality education?

That week I received many phone calls from angry alumni who thought our president ought to be fired, along with the athletic director. It was obvious – at least by what was written in the newspaper – that our priorities were mixed-up.

Lost in all of the spin was the reality of the situation. That being, SDSU has twice as many academically gifted students as does the "Ivy of the Plains." It is fact, not glossy spun opinion.

Need proof?

Opportunity Scholarships are offered to high school seniors by the state of South Dakota. To qualify, a student must attain a score of twenty-four or higher on his or her ACT examination. In the fall of 2008, 461 of those freshmen students enrolled at SDSU. In comparison, 239 attended USD.

That would be double.

Even the *Argus Leader* article in 2002 noted that more than seven hundred freshman students at SDSU had ACT scores of at least twenty-four, while the USD freshmen class had only 357 who hit that mark.

Again, that would be double.

Now, I'm not a math major. But it seems to me that if every year, SDSU harvests two times as many of the brightest kids in the state and region as does USD, pretty soon you would have to assume we have twice as many smart kids walking around our campus.

It gets better. The Dakota Corps Scholarships, elite academic awards worth more than six thousand dallars a year and given by the state of South Dakota, go to the top students in the state. In 2008, a total of sixty students gained the distinction. Forty of those students enrolled at SDSU – eight went to USD.

Ah, that would be quintuple.

We don't run around and brag about these things. Like a glacier, we quietly move along, slow but steady, doing our business, just getting the chores done.

I'm reminded of a moment I had at the old South Dakota Governor's Mansion a few years ago. Governor Bill Janklow, a USD alumnus, had asked the alumni directors from the public universities to attend a luncheon.

At the outset of the meeting, we took turns introducing ourselves. After I said who I was and where I came from, Governor Janklow interrupted me and said, "What is it about your place? I've met so many people who flunked out after a semester or two, but will stand up and sing the college song as if they were the valedictorian of their classes!"

I believe it's called loyalty, sir. We have a lot to be proud of.

As for many USD alumni, I think their attitude toward us boils down to insecurity. They can't handle the truth about the success of SDSU. So, they feel a compelling need to take personal shots at us – questioning our intellect and making fun of our agricultural background. Mention of the latter awakens my anger.

In their reasoning, by putting us down, they can somehow lift themselves up. Former First Lady Eleanor Roosevelt said it best, "No one can make you feel inferior without your consent."

Well, USD faithful, you don't have our consent.

I'll get off my soapbox now and end with a story courtesy of the late radio legend Paul Harvey. He shared this many years ago on one of his broadcasts and I've never forgotten it. I hope you remember it, too.

Dr. Theodore Abercrombie was one of the most respected professors on campus. Students flocked to his classes. Even though he was coming to the end of his teaching career, young people sought his wisdom.

On the first day of class during the last semester before Dr. Abercrombie retired, he encountered a young man who challenged him several times during his lecture. It didn't stop there. Each time the class met, the petulant youngster argued with Dr. Abercrombie. Other students squirmed in their seats, uncomfortable at what they were witnessing.

Toward the end of the semester, a young lady approached Dr. Abercrombie after a particularly contentious class and said, "How can you let him get by with that? He's trying to make you look stupid."

The old professor smiled and said, "On the night of a full moon, somewhere on a prairie hillside sits a coyote. That coyote will howl and howl at the moon all night long. He'll stop for a moment, dig at the dirt, and then start howling again. He thinks he's bigger, smarter and tougher than the moon. And, do you know what young lady?"

She replied, "What?"

Dr. Abercrombie paused for a moment and said, "Even with all that howling and carrying on, the moon shines just as bright."

That Great Big Beautiful Band

A presidential inauguration *is* a big deal. Even if your candidate isn't the one being sworn into office, it's a special time to celebrate all that is good about America.

And, if you are lucky enough, you might even find yourself on the grounds of The Mall in Washington, D.C., listening to the presidential oath being administered, then hearing a 21-gun salute fired by unseen, distant cannons. With every volley and waning echo, your emotions fill you with the awe, splendor and power of the moment.

Thanks to the Pride of the Dakotas Marching Band, I was able to witness the great democratic spectacle on January 20, 1997.

It started with a phone call to Pride director Jim McKinney on Sunday, November 3, 1996. A member of President Bill Clinton's campaign team contacted McKinney, requesting the band play at a rally in the Sioux Falls Arena the following night, the eve of the national election. It would be Clinton's last campaign stop as a candidate for president – ever.

Less than twenty-four hours later, band members filtered into the Arena. They were instructed to drop off their instruments in a secluded room so that members of the Secret Service could inspect them for possible weapons. Specially trained dogs sniffed their way through the piles of trombone, trumpet and clarinet cases.

Then, McKinney said, "A dog went crazy and started howling over a tuba case." Secret Service agents hovered around the tuba case, and after assessing the situation, carefully opened it.

Instead of a gun, they found Cheetos. Yes, the yellow, crunchy cornmeal snacks. A tuba player had left a bag of Cheetos in the case. One of the Secret Service agents said Cheetos were used as rewards for the dogs.

With the tuba and other instruments gaining security clearance, the Pride entertained the packed house of more than five thousand people for the next few hours, waiting for President Clinton to show up. They played every song they knew because Clinton did not arrive until 12:30 a.m. McKinney laughed and said, "They even played some things they didn't know."

After Clinton's remarks, the master of ceremonies asked everyone in the arena to leave but told the Pride members to remain seated. A Secret Service agent came forward and said President Clinton wanted his picture taken with the band. As soon as the crowd cleared, the president appeared. The band cheered and McKinney presented Clinton with a Pride baseball cap.

A few moments later, Hillary Clinton and daughter Chelsea came into view. President Clinton introduced his wife. Then, the band members shouted out in unison, "She's a neat gal!" Hillary smiled.

The picture was taken and as the president was leaving, the band started chanting, "Inaugural parade...inaugural parade...inaugural parade!" Clinton took off the

Pride cap and started waving it in unison to the chant. Then he said, "Sounds good to me!"

It sounded good to Jim McKinney, too. After Clinton easily defeated Senator Bob Dole, McKinney completed the lengthy inaugural parade application, sent it in and waited. Then, he waited some more.

In the meantime, McKinney asked me if the SDSU Alumni Association could assist in fundraising efforts, provided the band received an invitation. I jumped at the chance, realizing it was a fantastic opportunity for the students, university, alumni and the state of South Dakota.

If invited, the trip would cost around one hundred twenty thousand dollars. SDSU President Robert Wagner secured a gift of twenty thousand dollars from the Griffith Foundation, which was quickly matched by other sources. Each student was responsible for raising three hundred dollars. In 1997, there were only two hundred twenty members in the band.

We hatched a plan to have each student sell twelve T-shirts for twenty-five dollars each. A design was created with the words "The Pride is Back in Washington, D.C." The band had played for Ronald Reagan's inauguration in 1981 and we thought it appropriate to acknowledge that moment.

Time ticked away and there was still no word from Clinton's inaugural committee. That left us in a tough spot because the students were about to go home for Christmas break and we thought we were losing the optimum time to sell the shirts. So, we gambled and ordered them anyway. Three thousand shirts showed up during finals' week and we passed them out to the band members at a mass meeting in the Christy Ballroom.

A couple of industrious members immediately hit main street in Brookings. One of their stops was at *The Brookings Register,* the city's newspaper. Seizing on a good story, a reporter called President Wagner for comments.

The next thing I knew, I was being summoned to the president's office. He wasn't happy and I could understand why. As we hadn't yet received an official invitation to the parade, he was blindsided by the reporter's call. Plus, the passing out of the T-shirts may have been premature and there was great potential to embarrass the university. Thankfully, the invitation came a few hours later.

I dodged a bullet on that deal.

It was twenty degrees below zero on the morning we left for Washington, D.C. – January 17, 1997. The ever-present South Dakota wind took the biting chill past the minus forty degree mark. Two of the six buses "froze up" on the way to Brookings from Sioux Falls. But, like everything else during the horrible winter of 1996-97, you took it in stride.

Within hours of completing our tortuous twenty-eight-hour bus ride to the nation's capital, we had to quickly stretch the cramps out of our legs and get to a big party hosted by Al Neuharth, a South Dakota native and founder of *USA Today.* Senator Tom Daschle had asked Neuharth, a USD alumnus, to entertain a gathering of SDSU friends and alumni. More than five hundred people showed up.

In his remarks to the assembled throng, Neuharth said to the students, "You are in a college environment far better than anything you could get in one of those so-called fancy Ivy League schools. If you can make it at SDSU, you can make it anywhere."

In a stroke of good thinking, McKinney had taken the band members to an all-you-can-eat pizza buffet before going to the party. So instead of a mass of young people descending like vultures and gorging themselves on the wide variety of hors d'oeuvres, they were reduced to taking pictures of the tables filled with fancy treats. It was a pretty good trick.

The following day, the eve of the inauguration, McKinney and the assistant directors attended a meeting at the War College. Specific instructions were given to each entity involved with the parade. Since the Secret Service was involved, their word was law. For instance, there would be no wood rifles. It would be too easy to convert them into actual weapons.

Plus, it was absolutely forbidden for any unit to stop in front of the Presidential Reviewing Stand. No exceptions.

Early on the morning of January 20, the band headed to a staging area at the Pentagon. A busload of parents and supporters headed to The Mall to watch the swearing-in festivities. We stood a half-mile away from the Capitol Building with a mass of humanity in front of us. As we couldn't see anything but the backsides of people in front of us, we were forced to watch the entire ceremony on a huge projection screen.

The images were a little fuzzy and the sound quality wasn't great. But, you felt it a privilege just to be there.

After it was over, we headed to our assigned bleacher seating on Pennsylvania Avenue to watch the parade. We waited for three cold hours. It was twenty-five degrees, balmy conditions considering what we had left behind in South Dakota, but after awhile the chill numbed your entire body – you didn't want to move because it hurt

As we later learned, a traditional inaugural luncheon is held immediately following the swearing-in ceremony. The president, members of Congress and high-ranking government officials attend the event. There are plenty of toasts, speeches and giving of gifts. They tell each other how wonderful they are. One day you are a jerk, on inauguration day you are a great American leader, and the next day you go back to being a jerk again.

In the meantime, thousands of shivering people are sitting on cold bleachers waiting for the parade to begin.

Along about 2 p.m., uniformed officers took up positions, a few yards apart, on both sides of Pennsylvania Avenue. Police snipers appeared on rooftops. It was unnerving to see all that security, yet it was comforting to know the parade was imminent.

Finally, around 3 p.m., the president's limousine came gliding down the street. Surrounded by Secret Service agents, the huge vehicle crawled along and people sitting and standing on the parade route clapped. For many, it would be the closest they would ever get to the president of the United States.

So, it was a bit of a disappointment that you could not actually see the president. The tinted windows on the limousine prevented us from viewing President Clinton and the First Lady.

It seemed like you were just clapping for a nice car.

No matter, we were there because of the band, but it would be another hour before they passed our location.

We heard them before we saw them. Jim Coull, the assistant band director, had written a fanfare titled, "Inaugural Hymn." It is a powerful piece combining elements from "We Shall Overcome" and "The Battle Hymn of the Republic." I get goose bumps whenever I hear it – even to this day.

Director McKinney knew our location and made sure the band was in top form when they went by. We stood and cheered. Tears ran down the cheeks of many of the faces in our group. An enormous sense of pride washed over us, knowing we were at an important place at an important moment. The long bus trip and freezing temperatures were forgotten. Talented young people from our university were making us proud of who we were and where we came from.

The next day, newspapers and television shows were filled with highlights of the parade. Sadly, one band got all the coverage. That being the Florida A&M "Marching 100 Band." Ignoring the stern warning from the Secret Service, the band stopped in front of the Presidential Reviewing Stand and promptly broke into a rendition of the then-popular "Macarena" song and dance.

It seemed to me it was positive reinforcement of negative behavior. They broke the rules, yet got all the publicity.

After we got back to Brookings, McKinney asked President Wagner how he thought the band performed. Wagner said, "It was a toss-up on who had the best band. I didn't know if it was 'The President's Own' Marine Band or the Pride. I finally concluded that, indeed, the Pride stole the show."

I think so, too.

Liberation Day

In the beginning, they didn't like each other very much. Athletic competition, especially at a young age, will do that to you.

Dave Peterson and Doug Miller were eleven years old when they saw each other for the first time. It was at a YMCA basketball tournament and Dave's team from Rapid City, South Dakota, was playing against a group of youngsters from Sturgis, South Dakota. Doug was the star of that team.

"(Doug) was good, confident and a big guy for his age. He had more skills than any of us. So, I didn't like him," Dave said with a laugh.

The bad feelings spilled over into the summers. On the baseball field, Doug and Dave pitched for their teams. Batting became a test of courage. Dave said, "We threw at each other on purpose. I never hit him but I know he hit me."

They couldn't avoid each other. Over the next few years there were plenty of football and basketball games. With every bone-jarring tackle or hard foul, the dislike deepened.

Ironically, the athletic arena – where their competitive natures drove them apart – also brought them together. It was the summer before their junior year in high school when they played on the same baseball team. A conglomeration of young gifted athletes banded together to play amateur baseball. Doug and Dave, no longer dreaded rivals, found themselves in the awkward position of having to cheer for one another. It broke the ice.

By the time they were seniors in 1987, colleges were courting both of them. Dave visited Augustana College, the University of South Dakota and South Dakota State University. "I knew where I wanted to go," Dave said.

His dad, Doug Peterson, had been a three-sport star athlete at SDSU and was eventually inducted into the Jackrabbit Hall of Fame. He cast a long yellow and blue shadow in the Peterson household.

The choice wasn't so easy in the Miller home. Doug had offers to play football at SDSU and USD as well as a scholarship offer to play basketball at the Air Force Academy. But, Doug learned that because he wore contact lenses, he wouldn't be able to be a pilot. "Why would I join the Air Force if I can't fly?" Doug told his mother, Colleen Miller.

"In high school, the sport he was noted for was basketball, but he really loved football. I know he never regretted the decision he made to go to SDSU," Colleen said.

Dave and Doug would be teammates for the next five years. The first year they were "redshirted" – a term coined by college athletics for delaying an athlete's participation in intercollegiate sports. It is a year of weightlifting, building muscles and gaining some pounds.

Still, they had to join the full squad for practices. Dave, the recipient of a two hundred dollar scholarship, said he didn't know where he belonged in the beginning.

"After three days, one of the coaches looked at me and said, 'Who are you?'"

A year later, both would start for the Jackrabbits. It's a rarity to be a four-year starter for any college football program but those guys were good. Dave was in the defensive backfield and Doug played linebacker.

In their first game, in September 1989, Doug displayed the skills that would eventually attract the interest of NFL scouts. He had twelve tackles and blocked a 38-yard field goal attempt in the waning seconds to preserve a 14-12 victory over Southwest State University of Marshall, Minnesota.

"He had a tremendous game. We were so surprised and so excited," his mother, Colleen, told me.

More late-game heroics by Doug preserved a homecoming victory in one of the strangest games every played at Coughlin Alumni Stadium. The two-day affair – yes, two days – began on Saturday, October 28. With 9:01 left on the game clock and SDSU leading Morningside by a score of 13-6, the game was suspended due to heavy rain and lightning.

Twenty-two hours later, the game resumed in front of a few hundred fans. Dubbed "Hobo Day II," Morningside scored a late touchdown and lined up for the potential game-tying extra point. Doug busted through the middle of the line, leaped high and knocked the football down. The Jacks won, 13-12. His coach, Wayne Haensel, awarded him the game ball.

"He had a 42-inch vertical leap," Dave said. "Boy, could he jump."

As years passed, Doug and Dave's friendship deepened. They even became roommates. On the football field, they seemed to play as one. "There were lots of plays when we were just in sync. We knew each other so well," Dave said.

They depended on each other, too. Reflecting on the brutal nature of the sport, Dave said, "Doug was as tough as they come. There were times after he hit someone real hard, he kind of blacked out. He'd grab my arm and say, 'Where do I go? Where do I go?' I'd just tell him, 'Rush!' "

In time, Doug and Dave would gain all-conference honors. Doug would be named a consensus All-American in his senior year. The San Diego Chargers selected him in the seventh round of the 1993 NFL draft. He was the 188th player taken that year.

With diplomas in hand, the two friends went in different directions. Dave went to Hartford, Wisconsin, where he served as an athletic trainer for the next five years.

Doug headed to the rough and tumble world of the NFL. In his second year, the Chargers made it to the Super Bowl. On January 29, 1995, his team lost to the San Francisco 49ers 49-26. A year later he was out of football – a victim of a knee injury.

Though separated by distance, Dave and Doug continued to talk. "He was good at keeping in contact with people," Dave said.

Doug's mother echoed that. Colleen shared the story about a woman who contacted the Chargers' front office requesting that a player attend her dad's 80th birthday party. Doug volunteered to go. It was supposed to be a brief visit but Doug ate cake, sang "Happy Birthday" and stayed awhile to visit. Later, the woman sent a letter to Colleen and said Doug "kept in contact with my dad until the day he died."

"He was good with older people and good with kids," Colleen said.

With his playing days over, Doug decided he wanted to be a football coach. He enrolled at the University of California at Berkeley and became a graduate assistant in their football program. Life was good.

In July 1998, Dave accepted a job in the San Diego area. He contacted Doug, who was in Sturgis celebrating his tenth high school class reunion, and they agreed that a quick vacation in Colorado would do both of them some good.

Dave and Doug met in Denver. They put Doug's Harley Davidson motorcycle in the back of Dave's pickup truck and headed into the mountains. Doug had heard there were big fish at a place called Deep Lake outside of Eagle, Colorado.

It took two hours to drive nineteen miles of rugged, switchback dirt roads. At the end of their tortuous ascent, they crested the top of a hill and in front of them was a spectacular green meadow, with the Rockies as a backdrop. Two guys on horseback were herding sheep. Dave and Doug watched in awe as six dogs worked the herd. At one point Doug quipped, "I wonder what the poor people are doing today?"

Soon, they arrived at a rustic campsite and pitched a large pop-up tent. Within fifteen minutes it started to rain – then hail. Worried that the hail would shred the tent, a decision was made to move it under some pine trees for protection. Doug said, "Don't worry, I'm good." With that, he reached inside the tent, grabbed the polyethylene floor with his huge hands, lifted it off the ground and began carrying it up the side of a hill.

The marble-sized hail intensified so Dave jumped into the truck. He watched as Doug set the tent down and turn around to come back down the hill.

Just then a bolt a lightning struck Doug on the left shoulder. The shock waves from the strike rocked the truck. After a moment of disbelief, Dave jumped from the pickup and ran to Doug's side.

"The ground was just buzzing. It sounded like the humming of an electric fence," Dave said.

Dave checked for a pulse – nothing. He started CPR with two quick rescue breaths followed by chest compressions. The roar of the hail and rain made it hard to hear, so Dave bent down close to Doug's face to listen for a sign of life – he was breathing!

But, within a few minutes he stopped again. So Dave cupped his hands around Doug's mouth, finished one breath and was about to give another when he felt a second lightning bolt hit.

There was a huge white flash and Dave found himself airborne. He was thrown through a small stand of pine trees, some twenty feet away and amazingly, landed on his feet. Dave looked down and saw burn marks on his knees where the lightning had passed through him and into the ground.

Stunned and groggy, he didn't have time to reflect on his good fortune of surviving the lightning strike. Instead, he went back to Doug's side. He grabbed him and pulled him away from the trees out into the open.

"We were getting hailed on hard," Dave told me. Dave jumped into the truck and parked it in the center of the road so that no other vehicle could pass. Then he sounded the horn, hoping anyone nearby would interpret it as a distress signal. Dave grabbed a blue tarp from the back of the truck, ran back to Doug, and threw it over the two of them as he resumed CPR.

Two vacationing EMT helicopter pilots from California who were camped nearby heard the horn and came running. They worked on Doug for more than an hour. "There was a point when you knew it was over," Dave said, still feeling the pain of the moment.

An ambulance showed up an hour and a half later. So did a rescue helicopter. But, it was too late. Doug was only twenty-eight years old.

"I think about him every day," Dave said. "That whole situation makes me thankful for what I have. I constantly search for my role in life. How do I continue to get better?"

In trying to make sense of the tragedy of losing his friend, Dave kept to himself. "I didn't go back to see my old college football teammates," he said. He didn't want to talk about it and worried that his old friends might treat him differently. So, he stayed away.

Doug's mom, Colleen, felt the pain that only a mother who has lost a child can know. "I had a hard time for five or six years. I didn't like football because it brought back too many memories." And, it's a hurt that never really goes away. "It's something you always feel – more sometimes than others," she said. She stayed away, too.

Then, as if pulled by an invisible hand, Dave, Colleen and the rest of Doug's family showed up in Brookings on September 13, 2008. They were surprised and grateful to see each other. SDSU was playing Western Illinois in the annual Beef Bowl game. Ten years had passed since Doug had died. It was time.

After the game, Dave stood near the north end zone. He was talking to old friends when his dad came up to him and said, "Come on, Bruce wants you to go out there." Bruce was Doug Miller's father.

Dave walked to the 50-yard line – to midfield – and joined Bruce, Colleen, and Doug's sister, Marne, and his brother, J.R. What happened next caught him off guard. Colleen looked at Dave and with an excited voice said, "Are you ready for this?"

Bruce pulled out of his coat a plastic Ziploc bag that contained ashes – Doug's ashes. He gently poured the ashes into everyone's hands. There was a brief pause, each person reflecting on his or her own thoughts. Dave was thinking, "I breathed into Doug his last breath, I held him when he died, and now I was holding his ashes in my hand. It didn't seem real."

Then, together, they threw the ashes in the air.

In a magical coincidence, the stadium's loudspeakers were blaring out the song, "Simply the Best," made famous by singer Tina Turner. A small light gray cloud hung motionless in the air at midfield. Underneath, family members hugged and cried. Dave did, too.

Doug was back home – on the football field he loved – where members of his family had watched him play. And, where two young men, who were once youthful rivals, became like brothers.

It was liberation day.

Charlie's Angel

In August 1998, I went on a mission to visit the daughter of Charles Coughlin, the first great benefactor to South Dakota State. After Coughlin's death in 1972, there had been little contact between the university and surviving members of the family. In fact, the trail had gone cold.

Coughlin graduated from State in 1909. He hailed from Carthage, South Dakota. Besides being an excellent student, he was a gifted athlete. Coughlin, by virtue of his athletic prowess and his gifts to his alma mater, became the first person inducted into the SDSU Jackrabbit Hall of Fame in 1967. After graduation from then-SDSC, he joined his old college friend, Stephen Briggs, in taking the Briggs & Stratton Corporation to great business success.

Coughlin gave us our landmark bell tower, the Coughlin Campanile. He also gave more than fifty thousand dollars for the football field, now named Coughlin Alumni Stadium.

As luck would have it, Coughlin's granddaughter, Sheila, visited the campus at the same time we were making plans to raise money to renovate the Campanile. The iconic structure was in terrible shape. It was embarrassing to give tours of the campus and walk by the Campanile and see crumbling steps and limestone flaking off the arches of the doorways.

Dick Coddington, an alumnus originally from Ipswich, South Dakota, suggested the Alumni Association undertake a fundraising project in conjunction with the SDSU Foundation's "Visions for the Future" campaign. We called our effort "Return to Glory." Sid Bostic and his late wife, Bonnie, agreed to lead the campaign.

So, granddaughter Sheila showed up at the right moment. She spoke at the kickoff of the fundraising drive in September 1997. It was a beautiful late summer day and the Campus Green was the perfect venue. Sheila also told us about her mother, Colet, the daughter of Charles Coughlin. And, Sheila gave me her mother's phone number.

It took me almost a year to summon the courage to call Colet. I felt a little uncomfortable about it. The last thing I wanted was to come across as a guy interested only in money.

The call was finally made and Colet, understandably, was a little wary about my wanting to visit. We agreed on a date and she concluded our conversation by saying, "You can have one hour."

She lived in a suburb outside Milwaukee. Funny, I can't remember the name of the town. I do remember driving down the tree-lined lane leading up to her home. After parking my car, I went to the door and rang the doorbell. Within a few moments, I was met by a middle-aged woman who told me she was the caretaker. She led me into a large living area and directed me to sit on a couch.

Left alone, I surveyed the various pieces of art on the walls and floor. They were the trappings of a well-lived life.

Within five minutes the caretaker came back into the room, pushing Colet, who was sitting in a wheelchair. I wasn't expecting this. But, I stood up, walked to her side and shook her hand.

Colet was a distinguished looking woman. She appeared to be in her early 80s. Her white hair was immaculately groomed. A blanket covered her lap and draped to the floor in front of the wheelchair. She said matter-of-factly, "I have diabetes and have lost both my legs."

After a few pleasantries, she looked at her caretaker and said, "Come back in one hour." Then, Colet looked at me and asked, "Do you have any questions?"

Anticipating this, I'd done my homework and pulled out my list of questions. With each question, the barrier between us softened. Her answers became longer and more animated. It was obvious she had loved and adored her father. And, her father had doted on her.

Two stories caught my attention. The first being Charlie loved Irish music. It was his heritage. On several occasions he had hired the Clancy Brothers, direct from Ireland, to perform at special parties. Colet said the members of the well-known singing group, in time, had become friends of the family.

The second story centered on a strike by Briggs & Stratton employees when Colet was a young girl. Even though tempers were on edge and bad feelings abounded, Charlie and Colet visited the striking employees at their picket line on Christmas Eve to take them food and gifts and tell them they were appreciated.

Exactly one hour into our conversation, the caretaker returned and said, "Is everything OK?" Colet smiled at her and replied, "Yes, leave us alone."

I spent another hour with her. She said she had never stepped foot on the campus of South Dakota State. That surprised me. She did say her family gave a considerable amount of money to Marquette University in Milwaukee and a building there – the Charles L. Coughlin Center, was named for her father.

Then came a moment I will always remember. She said her father was a terrific speaker and oftentimes "brought down the house." His favorite moment was to share a poem written by Charles Hanson Towne. Colet said the audiences would be reduced to tears as he spoke. Then, in a deep, Greta Garbo-like voice, she repeated the poem from memory:

> *Around the corner I have a friend,*
> *In this great city that has no end;*
> *Yet days go by, and weeks rush on,*
> *And before you know it a year is gone,*
> *And I never see my old friend's face,*
> *For life is a swift and terrible race.*
> *He knows I like him just as well*
> *As the days when I rang his bell*
> *And he rang mine.*
> *We were younger then,*
> *And now we are busy, tired men;*
> *Tired of playing a foolish game,*
> *Tired with trying to make a name.*
> *"Tomorrow," I say, "I will call on Jim,*
> *Just to show I am thinking of him."*
> *But tomorrow comes – and tomorrow goes,*
> *And the distance between us grows and grows.*
> *Around the corner! – yet, miles away...*

"Here's a telegram, Sir...
'Jim died today'."
And that's what we get, and deserve in the end;
Around the corner, a vanquished friend.

As I sat and listened to her, I marveled at what I was witnessing. It was a grateful daughter, coming to the end of her own life, reliving a cherished memory of her father. That poem was burned into her soul and meant more than any building or structure named in her dad's honor.

It was time to leave. She wheeled her chair to the foyer. As we stood there, I noticed a framed pencil drawing of her father that hung on a wall. It was a side profile, showing him from head down to mid-thigh. He was neatly dressed in a suit. His right hand held a cigarette, smoke rising from the ash tip.

Colet laughed when I pointed out the cigarette. She said, "My mother was upset with the first drawing. He was holding a cocktail. She thought he would look better holding a cigarette. Times change, don't they?"

Eight months later Colet died. I'm glad I made the call.

Hurling Critters and Stuff

"Who's got the rabbit...who's got the rabbit...who's got the rabbit?"

That was the cheer proudly shouted out in rhythmic cadence by Augustana College students whenever the Jackrabbits showed up to play a basketball game. It was a source of pride for the Augustana student body.

Somewhere in their midst, a student was waiting for the right moment to heave a dead rabbit onto the basketball court. Sometimes there was more than one rabbit, but you always knew there would be fur and blood on the floor before the end of a game.

Most of the time, the rabbits thrown would be of the cottontail variety. Jackrabbits, by their elusive nature, are tougher to catch.

When it happened, the students would erupt in a gigantic cheer. Then, their basketball team would be assessed a technical foul. I always felt sorry for their players. Arguably, Augustana may have lost a few games because of those technical fouls.

Such is the stuff of rivalries. There *was* a rivalry between Augustana and SDSU. Honestly, I felt it was more of a big deal to Augustana than it was to SDSU. It wasn't as intense as the rivalry between SDSU and the University of South Dakota. However, whenever Augustana sported competitive athletic teams, there seemed to be more interest.

Augustana is a very good college. Much like USD, they like to tout themselves as *the* academic institution in the state and region. Self-proclaimed superiority does not make it so.

But, let's go back to the basketball arena. There was a cheer by the Augustana students that always bothered me. It usually took place when the outcome of a game was clearly in the Jackrabbits' favor. In unison, their students would yell, "Go back, go back, go back to the farm!"

The underlying meaning was that SDSU was filled with dimwitted farmers. It was their way of "putting us in our place." I often wondered how many Augustana students came from farms and how they felt about making fun of where they came from.

Another cheer, shouted out from the Augustana student section when their team was way behind, was "That's all right, that's OK, you'll be working for us some day!" There went that superiority thing again.

Now, SDSU students weren't exactly angels in this rivalry either. I remember the night the SDSU Drumline played a halftime performance at Frost Arena when the Jackrabbits hosted Augustana. I'm not sure how they did it, but halfway through their performance the drummers pointed their drumsticks at the SDSU students and the students yelled, "Augie sucks!"

As I was working in the athletic department at the time, I stood in a corner of the basketball floor, near the Augustana fans. Since I was wearing a sport coat and tie, looking official, I became a lightning rod for angry Augustana boosters. They were hot and let me know exactly what they thought.

A defining moment for me came in one of our last meetings with Augustana, prior to our jump to Division I. The games were held at the Elmen Center on the Augustana campus. I stopped at the ticket booth to pick up my tickets. The young woman who handed me my tickets was wearing a T-shirt with the words "Hate State" written on it.

At that moment I thought, "Over half the people attending this game will be from SDSU and you want to insult your customers?" I didn't say anything to her. Then, I proceeded toward the arena only to be greeted by a ticket taker wearing the same shirt. Right behind the ticket taker was a student selling game programs. Yes, that student was wearing one of those shirts, too. Still, I didn't say anything.

During the intermission of the women's game, we went to the concession stand. Kelly, my then 16-year-old-daughter, was with me. I stepped up to the counter ready to place my order and noticed every student working in that concession stand was wearing a "Hate State" shirt. It made me very angry. But, before I could say anything, Kelly said, "Dad, why are they letting them wear those shirts?"

Exactly. My 16-year-old could figure it out, but somehow the folks in Augustana's athletic department could not.

I wrote a letter to Dr. Bruce Halverson, president of Augustana College, sharing my thoughts about the experience and including my daughter's comments. Two days later, Dr. Halverson called me at the alumni office. His first words to me were, "We just don't get it." He apologized to me, asked me to extend his apologies to my daughter, and said he was going to do his best to make changes.

Dr. Halverson is a classy guy. He didn't have to call me. It would have been easy to simply write a letter. But, he took the extra step and I admire him for it.

And, he's a man of his word. The following year, the last time we played basketball at Augustana College, there were no ugly shirts.

Here's a final note on the dying art of hurling dead animals. Most fans wondered how the students could sneak those carcasses into the arena without being caught. It seemed the Augustana athletic department was doing a good job of searching fans for possible rabbit contraband. Even during the games, Augustana officials were constantly watching the student body looking for signs of potential trouble.

It was after my employment with SDSU that I found a source for the dead rabbits – the cheerleaders. Several of them have told me that they would sneak the rabbits into the basketball facilities by sticking them into their megaphones and covering them with their pompons. No one ever suspected a cheerleader as a culprit, thus the megaphones were never checked.

So, who's got the rabbit? The cheerleaders.

Sentimental Journey

In December 1926, George Frandsen borrowed twenty-five dollars from his brother, then boarded a train and headed west.

Thirty-four days and ten-thousand miles later, George returned to Brookings with two dollars in his pocket. During his journey, the 19-year-old rode the rails, sailed the high seas, played in two football games, and met a coaching legend.

Now, *that's* a road trip.

In November 1995, I sat down with George at a restaurant table at the Drake Motor Inn in Watertown, South Dakota. At the time, he was 88 years old. George stood no more than five-feet, seven-inches tall. And, he didn't weigh more than 160 pounds. It was hardly the stature of a football player, at least by today's standards.

But that is what he was, or rather, used to be. In 1926, George, a native of Plankinton, South Dakota, was a sophomore and played defensive back for the Jackrabbit football team. I'd met him on an earlier trip to Watertown and he had shared tidbits about the exploits of the 1926 team. It intrigued me and I wanted to know more. So, I called him and asked if I could take him to lunch.

The waitress stopped by our table, gave us menus and told us about the special for the day. George said to me, "I'm not very hungry." I told him to get what he wanted. When the waitress returned and asked George for his order, he said, "I'll take the special. Oh, and I want a hamburger, too." At that moment I wondered what he would have ordered if he had been hungry.

For the next two hours, George became young again. Energized by memories burned deep into his mind, he grew louder and more animated with each passing minute. Soon, all the patrons in the restaurant were looking our way.

I shrugged off the initial embarrassment of the moment and listened. For two hours I smiled. I was watching an 88-year-old man transform into a 19-year-old college student before my very eyes.

Even after the food was brought to our table, George ignored what was in front of him and kept talking. He was too excited to think about eating.

George's coach was the legendary Jack West. According to George, "West hated losing more than any guy I knew." The 1926 team didn't lose a game – at least not in 1926.

Late in the 1926 season, after beating Detroit University, West told the players if they beat their next opponent, St. Louis University, he would wire a friend in Hawaii to see if the Jackrabbits could play a few games there. Following the Detroit game, the team took a train directly to St. Louis.

George said the travel was hectic that year. "It seems all we did was play football and take trips," he said.

After beating St. Louis University 14-0, the team headed home wondering if the telegram Coach West sent fell into friendly hands. George said the coach told the players to check in their equipment and hit the books.

The wait wasn't long. Coach West pulled the team together and told them the good news. But, only twenty people could go on the trip. And, West's wife insisted she would be one of the twenty. George was hoping he would make the trip but two things might stand in his way: the limited number of players and his need for written permission from his parents because he was only 19 years old.

"I didn't know if I would be able to go," recalled George. "My mother wasn't too crazy about football and my dad had to talk her into it."

With permission granted, George and his teammates boarded a train in Brookings on December 11 and headed for San Francisco. From there, they took a ship to the Hawaiian Islands. The rolling waves of the ocean weren't kind to the flatlanders. "Some of the guys got sicker than horses," George said.

On the same boat, the USS Wilhelmina, was Knute Rockne, the famous coach from Notre Dame. Rockne and his wife were on vacation following a Fighting Irish game against the University of Southern California.

The State boys gathered around Rockne as he sat on a deck chair. George said, "He drew up plays. After he finished a play, he would hold it up and say, 'What do you think of that one boys!'"

Ironically, Rockne would see the young men again. He refereed both football games the Jackrabbits played in Hawaii.

After landing in Honolulu, George said the biggest problem was hunger. "We couldn't get enough to eat because the portions of Chinese food weren't large enough."

On Christmas Day 1926, the Jackrabbits played the University of Hawaii and won 9-3. All points were scored on field goals. Before the game, Coach West issued the team another challenge. "Coach said if we defeated Hawaii he would take us to Waikiki Beach," George said. At the beach, George bought three ukuleles and one grass skirt.

One week later, on New Year's Day 1927, the Jackrabbits played a "town team" from Honolulu. Perhaps tired from all the travel or weak from too little food, the State boys suffered their only defeat of the season, 13-12. *The Brookings Register* reported the game was played, "...under a broiling sun before a crowd of 12,000 ukulele players, dusky maidens and a sprinkling of Americans."

Then came the long trip home. On January 15, 1927, the team arrived in Brookings to a hero's welcome. Handshaking, backslapping, speeches and the college band playing "The Yellow and Blue" all greeted the tanned, weary travelers.

George took a bite from his now cold hamburger and thought about that long-ago moment. He got misty-eyed and said, "We were all so young – but boy, we were something," his voice trailing off.

Remembering Warren

"My dad wants you to give the eulogy at his funeral."

The voice belonged to Tom Williamson. We were college acquaintances at SDSU in the mid- to late-'70s. His father was Warren Williamson. After fighting a lengthy battle with cancer, his dad was near the end. I told Tom I would be proud to give the eulogy.

Warren was a native of Hurley, South Dakota. He was a terrific athlete and, like kids in most small towns, played all the school sports. After graduating in 1945, he spent a short stint in the Army. He enrolled at Kansas State University but soon realized he wouldn't see much playing time for the Wildcat football team. So, he transferred to South Dakota State.

As a Jackrabbit, he was an all-conference football player. His play even drew the attention of legendary Chicago Bears coach George Halas. But professional football was not in the cards, so after five years of coaching and teaching in Clear Lake and Winner, South Dakota, he returned to his alma mater in 1956. He was hired as intramural sports director, freshman football coach and wrestling coach.

Warren was a pioneer. He made the Jackrabbits a wrestling powerhouse. On a larger note, he is considered the father of wrestling in South Dakota.

It was his vision that established the recreation program at SDSU. Add to that, he built the highly successful intramural program enjoyed by tens of thousands of State students for the past four decades.

That intramural program is how I first met Warren. I was involved with student government and attended a meeting of the Athletic, Intramural and Recreation Committee. Warren trotted out impressive statistics on the number of students involved with the flag football program. But, Warren said, teams could play a lot more games if the intramural football field had lights. His rationale was to take advantage of September and early October evenings, with the temperature being perfect for football games.

Warren and the students got lights. I think of Warren every time I drive past the intramural field on early fall evenings, lights ablaze and hoards of college students playing flag football.

There's a sign on the southwest corner of the fields reading, "Warren E. Williamson Intramural Fields." Most students walk by and don't notice the sign. He touched the lives of countless young people who don't even know his name.

I do, because I remember.

My last visit with Warren was at his home a week before he died. He sat on the couch, a blanket on his lap. His voice was weak but his mind was sharp. If he was experiencing pain, he didn't talk about it. What he did talk about were his memories. Warren remembered everything.

Athletes and athletic contests, gardening and family vacations – all woven into our final visit. He wanted me to know that he had lived a good life and was leaving with no regrets. As I listened to all this, I marveled at how he had scheduled things in his life. And, here we were, having a casual conversation over what I might talk about at his funeral.

As I got up to leave after a two-hour visit, Dorothy, his wife, said matter-of-factly, "We plan everything."

Warren died a week later.

He was a no-nonsense kind of guy. At times, he used some salty language and it added color to his description of things. It was always a treat when he stopped by to visit me in either the athletic department or the alumni office. He was a man filled with stories.

On one of those visits I reminded him of the time when Bill Cosby, the actor and comedian, had come to campus in the late '70s. Cosby used Warren's office before he performed in Frost Arena. It seems Cosby helped himself to Warren's phone, made several long distance phone calls, and left a half-smoked cigar on the edge of the desk.

I asked Warren what he did with the cigar, thinking it would be a great collector's item. Warren said he threw it in the wastebasket. Well, that isn't exactly what he said. But his colorful description of that cigar told me he wasn't pleased with Cosby's actions – celebrity or not.

It's one of the things I loved about Warren – he wasn't given to haughtiness. He always remembered where he came from. A lot of people don't, but Warren did.

Steel Mallets

E lvis died on August 16, 1977. The news came to me on the radio as I was driving south of Brookings on old Highway 77 in my 1969 Buick Wildcat. People tend to remember where they were or what they were doing when certain worldly things happen. Well, I was on my way to play croquet.

Yes, croquet.

It started early in the summer of 1977. Chuck Gullickson and John Bastian were two great college friends. Chuck was about to set off for law school at New York University. He was the SDSU student body president in 1976-77. John served two terms as the executive secretary of the South Dakota Student Federation. John and I had another year at SDSU ahead of us. The three of us were deeply involved in student politics and enjoyed each other's company.

Chuck was living on his parent's farm the summer following his graduation. John and I dropped by to visit one night. Earlier in the day, Chuck had been rummaging through stuff in his garage and found the family's old croquet set. He thought it would be fun for us to play.

None of us could remember the exact rules of the game, so we made up our own.

There must have been a dozen rounds of croquet played that night. We whacked croquet balls all over the bumpy, patchy grass in Chuck's yard. It didn't take long and we got hooked. For the rest of that summer we played croquet almost every day. When you are young you sometimes grasp onto different, goofy things.

During the last half of that summer, after a night at Jim's Tap, and still filled with the energy of the night, we would drive to the Campus Green and set up the wickets for a game of croquet. There was just enough artificial light produced by nearby light poles to see what we were doing. But, it was still hard to see the thin, wire wickets. So we tied toilet paper to the top of the wickets. Don't laugh – it worked.

As that glorious summer came to a close, Chuck, John and I vowed that the next time we would see each other we would play croquet. That meant a rendezvous with winter.

Thus was born the Greater Frozen Plains Croquet Classic.

On January 1, 1978, we descended on the Campus Green to play a round of croquet. We poured hot, boiling water on the frozen ground so we could drive in the wickets. A "poke and find" rule was implemented so that we could use the handle end of a croquet mallet while searching for a ball knocked under a layer of snow. You weren't allowed to remove snow, except for the revealing hole made by the poke. You had to blindly whack your way out of it.

Two hours later, we had our first champion – Chuck Gullickson. I looked in the trunk of my car for some type of trophy and found a frozen dead jackrabbit. I had shot it during the Christmas break. Chuck posed for pictures, proudly hoisting the rabbit over his head in a Wimbledon-like Kodak moment, then he promptly gave it back to me. I threw it back in the trunk of my car.

That was a big mistake.

A few months later I lost my entire set of keys, which included an ignition key and a key to the trunk. I had a spare key just for my ignition so I thought it didn't matter as I rarely used my trunk. In the meantime, I'd forgotten about the rabbit. Along about the end of March, I detected a bad odor coming from some place in the car. I looked under the car seats for rotting food, but I couldn't find anything. By the first part of April, I had to keep the windows of my car rolled down because the stench was unbearable.

Then, I remembered the rabbit. The locksmith about threw up when he opened the trunk of my car.

In the spring of 1979, Stan Marshall, then the athletic director at SDSU, asked us to consider holding a croquet tournament in conjunction with the Brookings' upcoming centennial celebration. Stan was an idea guy and thought that croquet, being an old-fashioned game, was a good fit for the upcoming festivities. Besides, Stan had played with us a few times at Pioneer Park and knew we were serious croquet aficionados.

Our first task was to take our made-up rules and write them down on paper. All players needed to understand "our brand" of croquet. We didn't have a name for the rules so we looked in the dictionary. To our amusement, Oliver Cromwell was a subject listed right before croquet. Thus was born "Cromwell's Abridged Rules of

Croquet Order." In other words, it meant nothing but it sure sounded like a fancy title.

When we sent the rules to Dr. Sherwood Berg, then the SDSU president, he sent a note back saying he didn't care for the name because of what Cromwell had done to the Irish. Ah yes, the response of an educated man.

Sixty-four people played in that first tournament. Four separate courts, each outlined in white chalk boundaries, were carved out of the Campus Green. Each court was adorned with new wood wickets. The wickets were painted in glossy white and really stood out in the green grass. Frankly, all of it was beautiful.

The individual courts bore the names of people we liked. Berg Court was named for President Berg. His assistant, Chuck Cecil, got his name on a court, too. Marshall Court honored our distinguished athletic director, Stan.

Our fourth court was named after Rutherford B. Hayes, the 19th president of the United States. We had discovered he liked to play croquet on the White House lawn, but even there the opposing Democrats would not let him alone. They charged he had squandered six dollars of taxpayers' money for a set of fancy croquet balls. He was a man close to our croquet-loving hearts.

We thought all the tournament players would be amateur, fun-loving types, just like us. That all changed when four guys from Watertown showed up.

They were professional croquet players. I swear it.

Each of them carried a black case – not unlike the iconic violin cases carried around by the Chicago mafia. Upon opening their cases, they pulled out what appeared to be steel broom handles and metal mallet heads. With a little bit of showmanship, they screwed the mallet heads onto the handles. And, when those guys hit the croquet balls with those new-fangled clubs, it produced an unearthly sound like nothing we had ever heard before.

It scared the hell out of us.

We got smoked. Everyone fell victim to steel mallet heads. The following year, as we were planning our second tournament, we decided not to tell the Watertown mob about it.

They found out anyway, showed up with their fancy weapons again, and completely destroyed everything in their paths. It was the last summer a croquet tournament was ever held on the Campus Green.

Fool us once, shame on you. Fool us twice, shame on us.

TOP RABBITS

I'm going to warn you, this chapter appeals to my chronic problem with Attention Deficit Disorder. No, a doctor didn't diagnose it. I figured it out in the fourth grade after I had spent three years learning nothing.

Just kidding – about the years – but not the disorder.

When I sat down to sketch out an outline of chapters for this book, I knew I wanted to dedicate a few words to presidents who I came to know. Some readers will be miffed that I didn't give more ink to their favorite person or shower more praise. My shortcomings aside, I will trudge on.

Presidents of colleges are interesting creatures. They practically give up their private lives, especially during evenings and weekends, to sit through hoards of boring banquets, attend a wide variety of events and run all over the country. Lethargic people who have oyster-like tendencies need not apply. A president is to be seen *and* heard. If they do not show up at a particular event, you hear the whispers, "Why isn't the president here?"

Yes, the pay is good, you get nice seats at basketball games and you are able to live in free government housing. But, the hours are long and you live in a fish bowl. Also, the position requires a person who speaks eloquently to legislators in the morning and still feels comfortable standing in a feedlot full of mooing cows in the afternoon. Fortunately, SDSU has had some terrific presidents. And, I might add, they have had good mates.

Hilton Briggs was a great man. He spent seventeen years at the helm of SDSU, preparing for and welcoming the baby-boom generation. Enrollment almost doubled and no fewer than eighteen major buildings or facilities were erected. It was an unparalleled time of growth and expansion.

Add to that, he faced the ugliness of campus unrest in the '60s and early '70s. Vietnam War protests had colleges throughout America on edge and SDSU was no exception. Briggs got a face full of fist, courtesy of an angry demonstrator in 1971. Still, he held firm and everyone knew who was in charge. There would be no monkey business on his watch.

I didn't get to know him on a personal level until he was almost eighty years old. He would drop by my office and talk about things – but never himself. Briggs was an incredibly modest man. Well into his eighties, you would see him at Beef Bowl and Pork Classic barbecues, wearing a white apron and pouring coffee for the guests. I always thought it was a special sight.

One thing that bothered him was that Dave Pearson never had a building named after him. Pearson was a special assistant and vice president at SDSU from 1959 to 1980. He was at Briggs' elbow for sixteen years and President Berg's for another five. As Briggs told me, "Dave Pearson was in the middle of every building project we had. He did most of the work and deserves some recognition." Since there's already a Pierson Hall on campus, named after Dean Edith Pierson, decision makers might think it would be confusing. Regardless, Dave Pearson loved SDSU and a lot of his sweat went into making the university a better place.

Sherwood Berg was the first SDSU graduate to return as president. He served from 1975 through the first half of 1984 and gave me my diploma. "Woody," as his friends call him, is brilliant and equipped with a terrific smile.

Honestly, I felt sorry for him. During his time as president, he was constantly challenged by the Board of Regents to cut programs. He didn't have a friend in the governor's chair either. It wasn't a fun time to be president.

I remember a Board of Regents meeting when the president of the School of Mines and Technology, without warning, stood and suggested that engineering programs be moved to Rapid City. It caught everybody by surprise.

The next day, Dr. Berg gave a presentation that showed SDSU graduates performed better on national engineering examinations than the students at the School of Mines and Technology. Plus, it cost less to educate our engineers. That shut all of them up.

A few months after I graduated from SDSU, my father died. Woody sent me a handwritten note offering his sympathies. His sister had just died, too, yet he took the time to write. Even to this day, whenever I see him, I think of that note and the act of kindness.

Ray Hoops wasn't president of SDSU long enough to buy a second bottle of Tabasco sauce. I met him in Leavenworth, Kansas, at an alumni event a few months before he "resigned." It seems some people have amnesia regarding what happened to him.

Robert Wagner was president from 1985 through 1997. He is one of the greatest speakers I've ever heard. I could listen to that man for hours. In the '70s, I took his very popular marriage class and it was a thrill to listen to his personal stories and apply them to the subject material. His lessons in storytelling have stuck with me – I learned from a master.

The university thrived during his tenure. He had the vision to ask alumnus Jerry Lohr, class of 1958, to spearhead SDSU's first major capital campaign. Jerry, a hard-driving and passionate guy, grabbed the SDSU Foundation with his wine-stained fingers and pulled it past the $50 million goal. He made countless trips between his wine vineyards in California and places around the country seeking gifts for his alma mater.

In June 2006, SDSU celebrated its 125th birthday with a big gala event. It's the last time I saw Dr. Wagner. He kissed me on my forehead. I liked it.

Peggy Miller became president in January 1998. A few months after her appointment, an older woman walked into the alumni office and said to me, "Only men should be presidents of SDSU."

It's safe to say that Dr. Miller proved her wrong. The students loved her. Plus, she could work a room better than anyone I've ever seen. Her charm and warm smile made alumni feel welcomed and appreciated.

She had a "can-do" spirit about her and wasn't afraid to take chances. SDSU's move to Division I athletics, a bold initiative, is one of her greatest legacies. Many critics have now been silenced.

One more thing about Dr. Miller – she enjoyed every minute of being president. And, it showed.

David Chicoine has now been given the baton of leadership. An SDSU graduate, he carved a fabulous career at the University of Illinois before returning to his alma mater. Add to that, he comes from a great family, which was honored as SDSU Family of the Year in 1986. In brief, he has the right stuff to be president. What I appreciate most is that he truly wants to be here.

By the way, for almost forty years there has been a quiet and unassuming woman who has been the glue in the President's Office. Linda Schumacher has been the secretary for six presidents. She wouldn't say it, but I know she has taught them a lot.

Next to being the governor, the SDSU president's position is the second most important job in state government. You administer the largest university in the state, push countless research projects and oversee an extension program that reaches out to every county in South Dakota. And, you've got to make a lot of people happy. It's a big job.

If you don't agree with me, well, write your own book.

My Original Dr. Phil

He always called me Vincent.
The *he* was Dr. John P. Hendrickson, head of the political science department from 1967 to 1988. Colleagues addressed him as J.P. Friends called him "Phil."

Few people have ever used my given name to address me, not even my parents. Once in awhile, when my mother got really angry with me, she would shout out "Vincent John!" In time, I associated Vincent with bad news. I didn't like bad news.

My grandfather adamantly disliked the name "Vincent," so my parents started referring to me by my initials shortly after I was born. I've been known by my initials all my life.

Dr. Hendrickson didn't know my grandfather.

In the classroom, while he spoke, you knew he was a brilliant man with a lot going on inside his head. At times, he seemed to want to spill out three ideas at the same time. I took two classes from him, "Mid-East and Africa" and "State and Local Government."

It was in "Mid-East and Africa" that I began to understand the complexity of that volatile region. So many people try to paint it simply as "good guys versus bad guys." The need for diplomacy is lost; big guns win.

I remember him talking about the 1973 Yom Kippur war between Egypt and Israel. The Soviet Union had troop planes in the air, headed for the war zone. President Nixon moved the United States to DEAFCON 3, our nuclear arsenal was readied, the Soviet planes turned around.

Instead of speaking softly and carrying a big stick, President Nixon boldly announced, "We backed the Soviets down!" Dr. Hendrickson did not like the showmanship. I remember his disdain for braggadocio.

His depth of knowledge aside, he was a very witty and funny man. One day in his "State and Local Government" class, a fellow student dropped a small plastic container and it rolled down to Dr. Hendrickson's feet. He picked it up, analyzed it for a moment and said to the student, "Is this where you keep your hypodermic needles?"

Occasionally he would pull a bag of candy out of his briefcase and pass it around in class. One day he held up a bag of treats, looked and me and said, "Vincent will be bringing in the candy on Wednesday." Then he paused for a moment and said, "Oh that's right, Vincent doesn't come to classes on Wednesdays or Fridays."

Busted.

One of my college friends happened to be Dr. Hendrickson's son, John. An embarrassing moment happened in March 1977, a few months before John graduated. There was a student leadership conference at Morningside College in Sioux City and I thought John was going to go with us. As I soon discovered, he wasn't planning to attend. Since John was living at home at the time, we stopped by the Hendrickson home a little after 6 a.m.

I rang the doorbell and waited. Nothing. So, I rang it again. The door finally opened and there stood Dr. Hendrickson, wearing a housecoat. Judging by the condition of his hair, I knew I had just woken him up. There was an awkward moment of silence, then Dr. Hendrickson looked at his wristwatch and said, "Vincent, breakfast won't be ready for half an hour."

Busted, again.

In the latter stages of his life, Dr. Hendrickson endured three major health situations. Twice he had heart bypass surgery. Then, in 2001, he had heart valves replaced. That one took its toll on him.

He had already spent a considerable amount of time at McKennan Hospital in Sioux Falls by the time I stopped by to visit in January 2002. Susie, his wife, thought it would be good for me to see him. After several minutes of scrubbing my hands, then dawning a hospital gown, I walked into his room.

Dr. Hendrickson was sitting in a wheelchair. He was tethered to several pieces of hospital equipment by wires and hoses. A white mist sprayed from the tracheotomy hole that was cut into his throat.

I didn't expect this. Dr. Hendrickson extended his right hand, which I shook, and he said, "Hello, Vincent."

For the next hour we talked about a variety of things. One subject was Tom Daschle, his former student who went on to become the United States Senate Majority Leader. I asked Dr. Hendrickson if he had had any inkling that Daschle would rise to such stature.

"I didn't have a clue," he replied. It was the same thing he had told Dave Kranz, the longtime political writer for the *Argus Leader*.

At one point during our conversation, a piece of equipment started beeping. Susie determined it to be the gadget attached to his finger so she tried to make an adjustment. "Ow!" Dr. Hendrickson cried out. Susie pulled back, thinking she was hurting her husband. A wry smile appeared on Dr. Hendrickson's face. "Oh you!" she said, giving him a slight whack on his shoulder.

It was time for me to leave. Frankly, it's an uncomfortable moment when you realize you might not see someone again. It doesn't seem real and you struggle for the right words. You don't quite know what to say.

We kept it simple. Dr. Hendrickson raised his hand. As I held it, he said, "Goodbye, Vincent."

I replied, "Goodbye, Phil."

THE HAT LADY

I never met Dr. Vivian Virginia Volstorff in person. I'd spoken to her on the phone a few times but I never sat and visited with her. I regret this.

She retired from SDSU in 1973 after serving the university for forty-one years, most notably as the Dean of Women. She was the last person to hold that title.

Since 1973, most SDSU students have come to know the Volstorff name, as it is associated with the ballroom in the University Student Union. The original ballroom was on the second floor of the building but when the facility was renovated in 2004, it took on a much larger form – now on the first floor.

Dr. Volstorff was twenty-five years old when she stepped off the train in Brookings in 1932. With a fresh doctorate in history from Northwestern University in Evanston, Illinois, she understood job scarcity in the early '30s and accepted the Dean of Women position at a salary of twenty-two hundred dollars a year. She hoped she could teach a little history, too.

One of her missions was to bring social refinement to the women attending a "cow college." To this end, she set in motion the idea of having freshman females attend something called a "cozy." Coeds would wear dresses, white gloves and sip on tea. That kind of stuff didn't happen much in Mud Butte, South Dakota.

She also was the driving force behind the spring ritual known as the Maypole Dance. On May 1 of each year, the ladies of the campus assembled at Sylvan Theatre on the Campus Green and danced around a maypole. That tradition ended with Dean Volstorff's retirement.

Shortly before she died, Dr. Volstorff's book, "The Winds of Change," was published. That book would not have become reality without the hard work of Dr. James O. Pedersen, one of her former students and colleagues, and his daughter, Jana (Pedersen) Petersen. The book does a great job of detailing the challenges Dr. Volstorff faced and her contributions to the history of the university.

There's a sense of sadness when you read the book. So many traditions are gone or have lost their luster. At one time, campus organizations worked countless hours to host events that framed the social network of student life and instilled loyalty and a sense of tradition. In brief, if you wanted to meet and socialize with fellow students, the place to be was on campus. Downtown bars and house parties have replaced much of that.

Like a mother goose watching over her goslings, Dr. Volstorff was fiercely protective of the well-being of female students, whom she believed were under her care. In "the old days," coeds had a curfew and at the appointed hour she would walk out the door of Wecota Hall and dangle her keys. That was a signal to the young lovers congregating on the steps of the dormitory that the doors were about to lock for the night. Intense kissing ensued for the next few moments.

Some students called those moments of passion "mush rush."

Over my years as alumni director, I had many older male alumni tell me that they had been Dr. Volstorff's escort at a particular dance. As she was single, Dr. Volstorff asked students to be her "date" at the various dance events on campus. At the time, it was a source of good-natured kidding by their college friends. But, as time has passed, Dr. Volstorff's "dates" have come to wear these memories as a source of pride.

In her presence, students addressed her as Dean Volstorff or Dr. Volstorff or Miss Volstorff. Behind her back, they called her VV or 3V or V-cubed. Mention of the latter brings many smiles as it mixes creativity with the language of mathematics – always the basis for good college humor.

No story about Dr. Volstorff would be complete without mention of her hat collection, which was sizeable. She made many of them. Her hats became her signature on fashion.

Bob Karolevitz, class of 1947, is a great writer and has a keen sense of humor. Writing in the 1947 yearbook, Bob said that Dr. Volstorff wore one of her hat creations to the annual Students' Association dinner and "...was jabbed in the coiffure (headdress) twice by a fellow who mistook her bonnet for his vegetable salad."

In a phone conversation with Dr. Volstorff, we talked about how the contemporary students had no idea who she was or what she did. Students recognize the Volstorff name as a place, not a person.

She told me she was in the grocery store one day and wrote a check for the purchase. The young female cashier noted the name printed on the check. She asked Dr. Volstorff, "Are you married to the guy who has that ballroom named after him?"

To which Dr. Volstorff replied, "I am the guy."

A Giant of a Man

Stan Marshall was an American success story. The Centerville, South Dakota, native was the athletic director at South Dakota State University from 1965 to 1980. He graduated from SDSU in 1950.

An only child, he lost his mother when he was seven years old. His dad, a plumber, raised him in a small flat connected to the back of the plumber's shop. Most meals he ate in the few restaurants around his hometown. He hitchhiked to college, carrying a spare shirt and pair of pants in his duffle bag.

From those humble beginnings, he rose to the top ranks of the National Collegiate Athletic Association – prestigious universities and big-time athletics. The National Association of Collegiate Directors of Athletics named him their leader in 1976. No small potatoes, that. His name, fittingly, adorns the athletic facility at his beloved SDSU.

By the time his fickle heart stopped beating at age fifty-three, he had gained legendary status.

Yet, almost three decades after his death, most people associate his name with a golf event. It's ironic considering he wasn't much of a golfer. The Stan Marshall I knew would find humor in it.

On a personal note, Stan is one of the reasons I was adamant about writing this book. Today, from Wall Street to Main Street, we constantly search for ethical leaders who are good role models – people who play by the rules. In Stan Marshall, I found good character in abundance. And, I want him to be remembered for more than just a golf tournament.

I asked Stan's wife of thirty-two years, Nona, if there was anything that really bothered him. She said, "He didn't like people who were untruthful. He thought if you lied and cheated on the small things, you were liable to lie and cheat on the big things, too."

My first meeting with Stan took place in September 1976. Harry Forsyth, the assistant athletic director, picked me up at the University Student Union and we drove to Stan's house. His heart was giving him some problems and he was at home recuperating.

Still, he was fully engaged, even in small matters. And, I went to see him because of a small matter. Stan had read in the school newspaper that the wrestling cheerleaders were upset because they weren't receiving funding. They wanted fifty dollars. Since I was serving as the finance chairman of the Students' Association, he wanted to know my thoughts.

That impressed the heck out of me.

A year later, he dropped by to see me in the Students' Association office. His mood was dead serious. He told me a talented student-athlete was caught cheating on a test. Then, he shared with me the consequences he was considering. "I'm not going to sweep this under a rug," he said. After outlining his concerns for the university, the general student body and the guilty student-athlete, he said, "What do you think?"

My answer was a stuttering mass of nothingness.

After he left the office, I sat in my chair absolutely amazed at what I had just experienced. He sincerely cared about what I thought.

In time, I learned he had a terrific sense of humor. Warren Williamson, Stan's friend and colleague, recalled the bus trips when they were teammates on the Jackrabbit football team in the late '40s. "He could imitate coaches and players. He'd have everybody rolling in the aisles," Warren said.

When the Cuban basketball team came to SDSU for an historic visit in November 1977, Stan asked me to give the official welcome just prior to the start of the game. I managed a poor attempt at greeting them in Spanish, their native language. A few days later, Stan sent me a note that read, "I thought I detected a smile or two on a couple of Cuban faces but I thought your presentation was delivered in the best Eurekan German-Spanish I have ever heard."

I've still got the note.

Stan also had an insatiable need to learn new things. Shortly after being named athletic director in 1965, he told Harry Forsyth, "You and I need to get our doctorate degrees." Well, they did. Nona Marshall told me she thought it was one of Stan's biggest accomplishments because it required so much time and the family had to move to Springfield, Massachusetts.

The quest for new experiences didn't stop at the classroom door. During a casual conversation with Harry one day, Stan asked, "Have you ever been to Nashville?" Harry said he hadn't. "Three days later we were on the way to Nashville with our wives. That was Stan – always on the go," Harry said, laughing about the memory.

On Saturday mornings, Stan enjoyed a ritual with another friend, Chuck Cecil. During breakfast at the old Ward's Café in downtown Brookings, they would conspire to set out on different, out of the ordinary adventures. "Heck, we went to farm auctions, or a sales barn to watch them sell cattle, or a drive around Oakwood Park – weird stuff like that," Chuck told me. Mixed in were things like Boy Scout bean feeds, a dog show or a 4-H Achievement Day event. "I think Stan enjoyed putting athletics aside on this day and being an ordinary person interested in things other than athletics," Chuck said.

Curiosity kept Stan digging, literally, even if it meant in garbage. Chuck likes to recall the time he and Stan were driving through Lincoln, Nebraska, and stopped at the University of Nebraska's Cornhusker football field. It was a miserable cold December day. Undaunted and coatless, Stan was on a mission.

"I'll always remember him jumping the fence at 'Husker stadium to dig through garbage cans at the football field and pulling out old game programs...looking for ideas to bring back to campus," Chuck said.

Stan was big on new ideas. And, one of his best was the Beef Bowl. He even had the foresight to have the name patented. Over time, some colleges have tried to steal the name but have promptly received a stern warning from SDSU about patent rights.

The dates of Stan's tenure as athletic director mirrored the rise of women's athletics on the national and local levels. To better understand the mood and thinking of women in sports, he and his assistant, Harry, joined the Association for Intercollegiate Athletics for Women. The group dissolved in 1982 but it was the national entity for women's athletics before giving way to the NCAA.

"I went to their conventions every year," Harry told me. "There was one other guy, me, and four hundred women," he added. Harry credits Jack Frost, athletic director at SDSU from 1947 to 1960 with placing both men's and women's athletics in one organization. Most institutions had separate departments for the men and women and it created a lot of dissension and bitterness.

Perhaps Stan's most visible accomplishment is the Health, Physical Education and Recreation Center, which bears his name. There were lots of trip to Pierre, letters and phone calls, rallying decision makers for the money.

The original plan included a fieldhouse on the north side of the athletic facility. But, when the final funding was announced, it was far short of what was needed. A decision had to be made – downsize the entire project or lop off the fieldhouse. Stan huddled with Harry and President Briggs and made a difficult choice: There would be no fieldhouse.

That decision was pure vision. Every time I sit in Frost Arena I look around at that grand facility and think to myself, "What if this place was only half the size?" Jackrabbit fans need to be grateful for Stan's vision.

Sadly, the same heart that made Stan love SDSU was failing him. A bout with scarlet fever as a youngster had left his heart damaged. In early 1980, he had to make another tough decision – this time about his health.

Doctors at the Mayo Clinic in Rochester, Minnesota, suggested a mitral valve in his heart be replaced. Stan had to decide between a mechanical valve or a new surgical option – a pig's valve.

On May 1, 1980, the mechanical variety started pumping blood in Stan's heart. As Nona described it, "It clicked like a clock. You could hear it." But, the palpitations – intermittent rapid beating of the heart – did not go away. Harry told me that when he went to visit him in the hospital, Stan said, "They sent a plumber to do an electrician's job." Today's pacemakers, which shock the heart back into normal rhythm, might have corrected the problem.

A month and a half later, Stan felt strong enough to attend the National Association of Collegiate Athletic Directors convention in Las Vegas, Nevada. Nona was with him. After going out to dinner, they retired for the evening. During the early morning hours of June 14, his troubled heart stopped beating.

The giant was dead. I still remember where I was and what I was doing when I heard the news. Like so many, I was profoundly saddened. I felt like I'd lost a good friend.

Today, almost thirty years later, I smile whenever his name is brought up. I think of his energy, spirit and sense of humor. Heck, I still remember a couple of jokes he told me. He was a terrific storyteller.

Most of all, Stan was a great teacher. He often spoke of "teachable moments." Athletic competition offers a special venue to learn life lessons. In his words, "It provides the opportunity to develop character or characters."

Through him, I came to understand the impact an athletic program has on the image of a university. Quality programs don't happen by accident. It requires a lot of hard work. There are long hours, miles of lonely travel and having to deal with difficult situations that come from being associated with young people. Then, there is the pain of losing games, especially to a rival school. That brings out the Monday morning quarterbacks. You have to deal with them, too.

In athletics, everyone is an expert.

Harry, who succeeded Stan as athletic director, told me a story that seems a fitting end for this chapter. It was the late '60s and the University of South Dakota was in town to play a basketball game in the infamous Barn. As usual when the two schools met, the fans were loud and raucous.

In addition to crowd control, there was something else to worry about that night. Some ingenious students had hung a dead coyote from the ceiling of the facility.

Stan and Harry, wearing ties and sport coats, quickly moved forward to remove the dead animal. Nona Marshall and Harry's wife, Charleen, were near some students who were watching the dilemma unfold.

They overheard a young man ask, "Who are those two guys?" A student chimed in, "It's the athletic director and assistant athletic director." The first student said, "What do they do?"

"Not a damn thing," came the reply. Harry thought it was funny. Stan did, too.

Promotions Gone Bad

I loved working on promotions during my six years in the athletic department and my ten years in the alumni office. It was always exciting to try new things. We bombed a few times, but the reward of seeing smiles on peoples' faces, especially children, made the challenge fun.

In January 1991, three months after I had accepted the fundraising and promotions job in the athletic department, then-Athletic Director Fred Oien and I flew to Knoxville, Tennessee, to visit with the athletic development staff at the University of Tennessee. We learned a lot on that trip.

While there, we watched a men's basketball game. I can't remember the University of Tennessee's opponent that night, but I do remember two promotions we brought back to SDSU. A real crowd pleaser was shooting T-shirts into the audience with a big slingshot. Later that year we included T-shirts in our newly developed corporate sponsor packages.

The second idea we thought was fun and safe. Leave it to college students to bring a different twist to things.

Anyway, it was the first time we had seen 3/10 cards. The placards were a little larger than a normal sheet of typing paper. On one side was a large, bold number 3. On the other side was the number 10. The idea was that every time a player from the home team nailed a three-point shot, the students and fans would hold up the card with the number 3 facing the court.

If someone from the home team knocked down a dunk shot, the faithful would hold up the number 10. Style or degree of difficulty didn't matter. A dunk was a 10.

Fast forward to our next basketball season. We handed out hundreds of our own version of the three/ten cards to the students as they walked into Frost Arena one night. It didn't take them long to figure out how to use them. Yes, we were pleased with the promotion – until intermission.

It just so happened that two female college students were honored during halftime activities. Each held some type of queen title and wore tiaras depicting her status. Unfortunately, the male college students felt the need to judge the young ladies, using the placards, as they were introduced.

The first young lady's name was announced and a sea of 10s rose in the air from the student section. I felt an immediate sense of horror, as I knew what was coming next. Sure enough, when the other queen's name came over the public address system the students responded by holding up 3s.

I felt sorry for the young woman and any family members who may have been in attendance. Nothing could be done but you can bet we never ran that promotion again with queens being introduced at halftime.

Frost Arena was the site of another learning experience. Tanya Crevier, an SDSU alumna and world-famous basketball wizard, was slated to perform during halftimes of both the men's and women's games.

Due to a conflict, she wasn't able to come in early to rehearse. Just before she went on, she handed me a cassette tape and instructed me to play it during her performance. "I want it loud," she said. So, we popped in the tape and the music started. Twice Tanya looked at me early on in her performance, still dribbling basketballs, and gave me a "thumb's up." That meant she wanted the music to be louder. She was used to professional arenas where people heard and *felt* the music. I had the volume as high as it would go and she was still giving me the thumb.

Mind you, this was the early '90s. It wasn't a sophisticated sound system and the speakers weren't properly aligned. In fact, the speakers were pointed to the upper deck of fans and the people in the lower level didn't get the same volume.

After a few minutes, I left the scorer's table to make a trip to the upper level. I was curious about how loud the music was upstairs.

Moments after I arrived, a man quickly approached me, grabbed me by the breast of my sport jacket with both his hands, and threw me against the wall – hard. Visibly angry, he yelled, "Turn that damned thing down!"

I was stunned. He was a retired and well-respected member of the academic community. It seemed so out of character. Yet, I could hear the music and it was too loud.

The next night the man apologized to me. I appreciated him doing that. But, it was a reminder of the importance of proper planning when doing promotions.

My first real foray into athletic promotions happened in September 1991. SDSU was scheduled to play its football home opener against the University of Nebraska at Kearney. As the entire athletic promotions staff was new, it was an opportunity for us to make our mark.

Plus, it would be Mike Daly's debut as head football coach. So, there was a lot of excitement leading up to the day.

Patriotism was sky high in America at that time. Six months earlier, the United States and a few allies had spanked Saddam Hussein in the first Gulf War, better known as Operation Desert Shield. So, we decided to honor the veterans of that conflict and include all those who had ever served in the military.

An enormous American flag was hung off the back of the cement bleachers on the west side of Coughlin Alumni Stadium. Just outside the gates we erected a tent. There would be music and food. This is commonplace today, but it wasn't in 1991.

The halftime show would feature the singing group, The Great Pretenders. The quartet was always a big hit at the Keltgen Seed tent at the South Dakota State Fair and we thought they were just right for us. Since the students who comprised the Pride of the Dakotas Marching Band had just returned to school and weren't ready for a field performance yet, we needed something special at halftime. The big finale would be The Great Pretenders singing "God Bless the USA" and veterans from all wars would unfurl a huge American flag. We were excited.

Plus, we planned a big deal just prior to the start of the game. Four parachutists would glide into Coughlin Alumni Stadium during the national anthem. The last guy to land would carry the game football.

Working with the folks from the ROTC department, there would be a man on the field with binoculars, watching the parachutists. At one thousand feet, the guy carrying the football (he had a wrist altimeter) would waive his arms. This meant he was one minute from being on the ground. There would be a signal to The Great Pretenders to begin singing the national anthem. It would take one minute to sing the song – meaning that the guy with the football would hit the ground at the exact moment the anthem came to its conclusion.

Big stuff and we had it planned perfectly, at least we thought. We hadn't planned on rain and it came in buckets.

Three hours before game time we were scrambling. The pre-game event with the tent was cancelled. A decision was made to delay the start of the game by half an hour. We brought the parachute guys into a meeting and asked them if they thought they could still make the jump. They were eager to do it.

Mind you, it takes four guys awhile to descend from a mile in the air, so everything depended on that last thousand feet. We were informed that the football team would come out of the locker room after the national anthem. Coach Daly wanted the anthem to be the focus at that moment, not the football team.

Fifteen minutes before the start of the game, the airplane carrying the parachutists flew over the stadium and you could see the guys jumping. They were on their way.

I stood there for the next few minutes and watched them gently float to earth. My heart was pumping hard because the big moment was at hand.

All of a sudden, the football team emerged from the locker room. That wasn't in the plans. I was in a state of full-blown panic. But, the reality of the situation was that it was the first game of the season and it had already been delayed. Those players were anxious to get going.

After jumping on top of each other in a mob-like frenzied fashion, the team stormed onto the field. Seeing this, the band immediately started playing the school song.

"Wait!" I yelled. But my words were shouted down by the noise and excitement of an unstoppable wave.

At about that same moment, the parachutist carrying the football started to waive his arms. He was at one thousand feet. But, since the band was in the midst of the school song, there was no way to begin the national anthem.

The first parachutist landed at about the same time The Great Pretenders finally started singing. And it wasn't pretty. Because of the rain, the grass was very slippery and the guy ended up on his rear end. The student section went wild.

Both the second and third parachutists met the same fate. The students cheered each botched landing. By that time, and because of the delay, the national anthem was already over. Nobody seemed to pay much attention to the song anyway.

Finally, the guy carrying the football hit the ground – and ended up on his butt, too. It was bedlam. The students were all high-fiving each other. It was the least reverent national anthem I had ever witnessed.

I learned two valuable lessons that day. First, you can't put parachutists back into an airplane after they've already jumped. And second, if you are going to try something that requires some timing, you need to practice it first.

The Year That Wasn't

It was a great team. Arguably, it may have been the most talented group of players ever to wear the Jackrabbit football uniform – at least on the offensive side of the ball.

The 1993 roster included two future NFL stars, one of which might end up in the Professional Football Hall of Fame. Another player was headed to the Canadian Football League. Toss in the first team all-conference quarterback and, at least on paper, it had all the makings of a conference championship, and with a little luck, a run at the national championship.

But, it was a weird year.

It started on a warm day in Missoula, Montana, in early September. Midway through the third quarter, the Jackrabbits were mauling the University of Montana Grizzlies, a Division I-AA school, by a score of 38 to 7.

I remember jumping up and yelling, "We're going to win!" When I sat down I felt a tap on my shoulder. I looked behind me and saw the smiling face of Dr. Loren Amundson from Sioux Falls. He simply said, "Remember the Stanford game."

The good doctor was referring to the 1982 football game between Stanford and the University of California-

Berkeley. On the final play of the game, with Stanford leading by a point and only four seconds left on the clock, Cal players continued to lateral the football back and forth. In the pandemonium of the moment, thinking their team had won, the Stanford band assumed the game was over so they ran onto the field. At about that same time, a Cal player carrying the football sprinted into the end zone and promptly bowled over a bewildered trombone player. Cal won on a miracle finish.

It was Dr. Amundson's way of saying the fat lady hadn't even started humming. Unfortunately, his words were prophetic as Montana scored forty-five points in the last eighteen minutes of the game. Each time they scored, a cannon would fire. It went off so much it started to sound like a machine gun. In the most emotion-filled game I've ever witnessed, we ended up losing 52-48.

When you talk to the guys from the 1993 team, that one still hurts.

As fans, we were energized by nearly beating Montana. Euphoria turned into cold reality, as in the next four weeks we lost to St. Cloud State and the University of Northern Colorado. Yes, we beat Southwest State and Morningside, but they were two below-average teams. The promise of a great season quickly wilted into an unimpressive record of 2-3.

Then came October 9. The much-heralded Bison of North Dakota State University came into Coughlin Alumni Stadium riding a seventeen-game winning streak over the Jackrabbits. We hadn't beaten them since 1975. So, there was a bit of surprise and enjoyment that for the better part of three quarters, SDSU was having its way with NDSU. Then, the Bison started doing their old Bison tricks. They started to rally.

I remember sitting in the press box. Ed Schultz, the voice of the Bison and a man of great ego – now a nationally syndicated radio personality – stepped out of his broadcast booth and said sarcastically, "Looks like the Montana game all over again."

My first instinct was to kick him. SDSU held on and won 42-30. The long Jackrabbit nightmare was over.

Instead of celebrating into the night, like most of the Jackrabbit fans, I had to go to Gigglebee's in Sioux Falls for my six-year-old daughter's birthday party. For two hours I watched a stuffed mechanical coyote ride around on a tricycle delivering pizzas to tables filled with loud children and haggard parents. I hated that coyote.

After trouncing the University of Nebraska-Omaha on Hobo Day, the next stop was the DakotaDome in Vermillion.

We scored first against the Coyotes and never saw the end zone again. With a minute and a half left in the game, USD scored a touchdown to make the score 27-7. They lined up to kick the extra point then promptly ran in a two-point conversion.

They were rubbing it in our faces.

It was payback time for the Coyote's head coach, Dennis Creehan. Three years before that, he had been one of three candidates for the top job at SDSU. Obviously still miffed that Mike Daly had been named the Jackrabbit coach, he was determined to get the last word.

Creehan was quoted in the next day's newspaper, saying there was a "miscommunication" on the play and the team was supposed to kick the extra point. Miscommunication my rabbit's foot – I think he did it on purpose.

Immediately following USD's two-point conversion, I had an out-of-body experience. It's true – I completely snapped. I ran down the steps of the DakotaDome shouting out every obscenity-laced phrase I could think of. All of it was directed at Creehan. About halfway down, I noticed Jackrabbit fans staring at me, aghast at what I was screaming. I stopped and thought, "What are you doing?"

It was the last time I ever watched SDSU play USD in an athletic event in the DakotaDome. On my drive home, I vowed never to go there again – at least not for an athletic event between the two schools.

The Jackrabbits would go on to win the next three games. A win over Augustana was followed by a 60-42 drubbing of conference co-champion Mankato State. On the last game of the season, SDSU hosted the other conference co-champion, the University of North Dakota. The Jack's defense allowed the Fighting Sioux only 154 yards of total offense. It was an old-fashioned thrashing and we won 28-0.

Thus ended a Dr. Jekyll and Mr. Hyde season with a record of seven wins and four losses. It was hard to figure out which team was going to show up.

Our quarterback, Todd McDonald, finished the season passing for 2,715 yards, then a Jackrabbit record. Dan Nelson, a grinding running back from Volga, South Dakota, ran for 1,150 yards. Future winner of two Super Bowl rings, Adam Timmerman, anchored the offensive line. Fleet-footed Dean Herrboldt from Freeman, South Dakota, was a threat at wide receiver and ended up playing professional football in Canada. Our tight end, Jake Hines, was named first team all-conference, and a year later, an All-American.

Added into the mix was strong-legged kicker, Adam Vinatieri, who currently sports four Super Bowl rings and has become an NFL legend for booting clutch field goals.

We had the offensive firepower.

The only player to be named first team all-conference on the defensive side of the ball was Jim Remme from Luverne, Minnesota.

Interestingly, it wasn't Remme's defensive prowess that has made him the answer to a great SDSU trivia question. The question: What defensive lineman replaced Adam Vinatieri in kicking extra points and field goals at the end of the 1993 season?

Yes, the answer is Jim Remme. He had to be the biggest kicker in America in 1993 – maybe ever.

At six-feet, two-inches tall and weighing 275 pounds, he looked out of place standing in the backfield. On his right foot, he wore a black, size twelve, specially built square-toed kicking shoe. Heavy wrappings of dirt and grass-stained athletic tape covered his arms, hands and fingers.

Appearances aside, the most striking thing was that he was an old-fashioned, straight-on kicker. No fancy soccer-style kicking for Big Jim.

So, what happened to Vinatieri?

"Adam was struggling," Remme told me. "He had the shanks and seemed to be losing confidence. I couldn't believe it. He was even missing extra points."

In the last four games of the 1993 season, Remme was called on to kick eight extra points and attempt one field goal. "I didn't miss any extra points," he said with a big grin. "I tried one 37-yard field goal at Mankato. It ended up in the corner of the end zone. My wife still gives me a bad time about that one."

Eventually, Vinatieri regained his confidence. He left SDSU holding most of the school's kicking records. Parker Douglass, a 2007 graduate, has since eclipsed those marks.

It's ironic that one of the greatest kickers in the history of the National Football League, a good bet for the Professional Football Hall of Fame, was never named first team all-conference for place-kicking.

Like the 1993 football season, go figure.

Making a Difference

Saturday, April 17, 1993, was one of the toughest days of my life.

SDSU was playing a baseball game at old Huether Field. I can't recall who we were playing that day but I do remember a sunny sky with a temperature hovering in the mid-'50s.

At some point I got called up to the press box. I climbed the metal ladder rungs and was immediately met by Ron Lenz, SDSU's longtime sports information director. The grim expression on his face told me there was a problem. He said that Wade Knutson, a star track athlete from Watertown, South Dakota, had been seriously hurt in a pole-vaulting accident while competing at a meet in Sioux City. The team had withdrawn from the competition and was on a bus headed for home.

Later, more information came from Sioux City. Evidently Wade became hurt when he missed the protective matting on his landing and hit the concrete. The back of his head took the brunt of the fall. He was in critical condition.

While I waited for the bus to arrive, I thought about Wade. He was a sophomore and just beginning to make his mark at decathlon events. To be a decathlon athlete, you have to be good at running, jumping and throwing. In other words, you need to be an all-around athlete. Wade was better than good and his body looked like it was chiseled from marble by a Greek sculptor.

Whenever Wade walked into the athletic department, he wore a big smile. He was always cheerful and greeted people warmly.

The bus carrying the track team pulled up in front of the Stanley J. Marshall building late in the afternoon. A few of the young people had already stepped off the bus by the time I reached it. I looked into their faces and saw horror and sadness. It was obvious they had witnessed something awful. After hugging a few of them, one young lady asked, "Do you know how Wade is?" I told her we had not received any new information.

That evening, a dozen or more team members gathered in the Ginn Trophy Room. Not knowing Wade's fate, they sensed a need to be together. Devastated from what they had experienced and watching the unfairness of life unfold in front of them, they needed each other.

Wade died later that night.

On Sunday, at noon, more than sixty team members met back in the Ginn Trophy Room. Any hope from the night before was now replaced by raw, agonizing grief. One by one, they took turns sharing stories about their fallen teammate. There were lots of tears and moments of laughter – the gamut of human emotion poured out of them.

The next day, Monday, brought more tragedy. National news showed images of the Branch Davidian compound outside Waco, Texas. After a fifty-one-day siege, the patience of federal authorities had run out and the complex was a complete inferno. Seventy-six people, all members of the religious cult, died in the blaze.

Later in the day, South Dakota Governor George Mickelson and seven others perished in a plane crash outside Dubuque, Iowa. Since the governor had lived in Brookings for many years, it hit the community especially hard.

It seemed like the world was unraveling. All of it left you numb.

Still, a few days later, two busloads of track athletes and coaches, almost a hundred in total, took the one-hour trip to Watertown for Wade's funeral. No one talked. It was a time for quiet reflection.

The track squad led the procession into the church. Up the aisle they walked, two by two, toward an altar filled with colorful flowers. I've never seen so many flowers at a funeral before or since.

Head coach Scott Underwood delivered a moving eulogy. I remember he spoke about building a wood deck at Wade's home. The coach wondered why they were using screws instead of nails. The project would go quicker with nails. Wade said using screws would be more work but the deck would last longer. No shortcuts – it was the right thing to do.

There's a lesson there for all of us.

Almost two decades have passed since that horrible time. Yet, in trying to make sense out the tragedy, I need to share two important stories.

The first deals with Justin Williams. He is Dr. Justin Williams now. In 1993, he was Wade's good friend and teammate. Justin, a graduate of Dell Rapids High School, was a Briggs Scholar, the highest academic award granted to SDSU students. In 1996, he graduated from SDSU with degrees in engineering physics and mechanical engineering.

At age twenty-six, Justin became the youngest doctoral candidate in bio-medical engineering in the history of Arizona State University. In brief, he's a genius.

Spurred on by what he witnessed on April 17, 1993, he has dedicated his life to studying the human brain and brain injuries. One day, Justin just might win the Nobel Prize for medicine.

Wade's mother and father, Ileen and Kent Knutson, shared the second story. It was a few weeks after Wade's death and they decided they wanted to establish a memorial in their son's honor. They came to my office, their faces showing the ever-present pain that just wouldn't go away.

In the middle of our labored conversation, they told me about a little boy by the name of Matt. Wade had met him a week before he died, while he was competing at a track meet at Northwest Missouri State University in Maryville, Missouri.

Smiles came to both Kent and Ileen as they described what happened. Matt was nine years old and stood about four feet tall. He was wearing a white T-shirt, blue jeans and a baseball cap. The toothy-grinned youngster wore large, round glasses and told Wade he liked the fact that Wade wore glasses, too.

Soon after arriving at the site of the track meet, Wade noticed Matt was shadowing him. They soon struck up a conversation. Matt said he was writing a paper for school and it was going to be about his wanting to become a decathlon athlete. That sparked an immediate bond between the two of them. Matt said he had tried to convince the school principal to buy him a javelin but he was told it was too dangerous.

During the course of the day, Matt imitated everything Wade did. If Wade stretched, jogged or jumped, pint-sized Matt mimicked his every motion. Even when Wade bent down to tie a shoelace, Matt repeated it.

Between the ten events associated with the decathlon, a contest Wade eventually won, the two new friends talked.

As the day was coming to an end, Matt asked Wade for his autograph. Wade complied, signed a piece of paper and handed it to the young lad. Matt carefully grabbed it, folded it neatly and treated it as if it was gold.

Then, the two shook hands and said goodbye.

I don't know if Matt ever found out Wade died. What I do know is this: Somewhere in the state of Missouri is a young man who remembers a beautiful spring day when a powerful athlete wearing the colors of my university took time for him. He made him feel important. And, he inspired him to pursue his dreams.

I'm proud Wade Knutson was a Jackrabbit.

A Capital Experience

July is always a hot month in Pierre.
Since the early '90s, the SDSU alumni faithful have assembled on warm, humid July nights, mostly at scenic Steamboat Park. The mighty Missouri River crawls along quietly in the distance. State government thinks it's the biggest thing in town. But, that river cut a path long before the city was platted and will be there long after the last bureaucrat breathes his last. The river has always been the biggest thing in town.

The largest crowd to attend an alumni event, at least in my memory, was the night Governor Mike Rounds and First Lady Jean Rounds, both SDSU alumni, hosted an event at the Governor's Home in July 2006. The five hundred alumni and family members who attended felt a sense of pride knowing that Jackrabbits occupied that important house.

For years, Paul Marso, class of 1974, coordinated the gatherings. After the refreshments, food and coaches' speeches about their upcoming seasons, several of the group would re-assemble in the back room at Bob's Lounge in downtown Pierre.

On the smoke-infested wood paneled walls in that back room hang numerous pictures of smiling people with big fish and various dead animals. Some of those pictures feature SDSU coaches and administrators proudly displaying their catches. As the biggest thing I ever caught was a lowly carp, I never made the coveted wall.

During a dozen of those years, SDSU coaches and staff were treated to world-class walleye fishing the morning after the alumni gathering. You've never lived life to the fullest until you've seen full-bodied SDSU alumnus Lowell Somsen take a backflip off his fishing boat. He makes quite a splash.

Vern and Debbie Brakke, both members of the class of 1975, hosted a fish fry on their boat that was docked at the marina at Spring Creek. There is something special about eating fresh, deep-fat-fried fish just plucked from the Missouri River.

Loveable Lowell Somsen was in charge of making margaritas. He added the ingredients and cranked the blender to life. After a few minutes, he stopped the blender, dipped his finger into the icy mixture, and gave it a taste test. Smacking his lips together a few times, he detected an imbalance in the concoction, and made the necessary additions. Once again, the blender whirred with excitement for half a minute and Lowell repeated his unique taste-test method. He then announced it was fit for human consumption.

Fresh fish and Lowell's margaritas are a winning combination after a warm day on the river.

The idea of having a Cereal Bowl during the SDSU football season came about during a fishing excursion in the mid-'90s. I was on a boat owned by Tom Gilsrud and Randy Englund. Good music is an essential component when you fish with those guys.

Somewhere between renditions of "Mac the Knife" and actor Lee Marvin's "Wandering Star," Randy asked if it would be possible to have an event to showcase the grain industries of South Dakota. He served as the executive director of the South Dakota Wheat Commission. And, he knew that cows had a Beef Bowl, pigs got a Pork Classic and sheep had their Lamb Bonanza. "Why not us?" he asked.

When we got back to campus, we checked to see if there was a registered trademark on "Cereal Bowl." There wasn't, so a new tradition was born – on a fishing boat.

My favorite Pierre memory occurred on a hot, steamy night in Steamboat Park. Black, ugly storm clouds were brewing to the southwest. There was no wind and the air was thick with humidity. Something was up – you just knew it.

Suddenly, Pierre's siren system screamed through the park. "Tornado!" someone yelled.

The alumni crowd quickly grabbed their belongings and started running toward the parking lot. All you could see in front of you were the backsides of people, young and old, in a hurry, heading to their cars and safety.

Surveying all of this, Scott Nagy, the men's basketball coach, said to me, "Do you have a camera?" I thought it was an odd question considering the perilous nature of the moment. Scott said, "You could take a picture of all those people running away, put it in the alumni magazine with the caption, 'This is what happens when you ask for money at an alumni gathering.'"

Funny stuff.

THE TIDY DEAN

I can't walk by a piece of trash lying on the grounds of the SDSU campus without thinking of Dean Allen Barnes.

Barnes was a sophisticated and educated man. When he spoke, you knew he belonged in a university setting. His sentences were perfectly aligned with appropriate pronouns and adjectives. And, he had a flare for dramatics that kept your interest. He was dean of the College of Arts and Sciences at SDSU from 1967 to 1985.

His communication skills aside, I remember Dean Barnes for his disdain of garbage. I am dead serious.

Every year, soon after student government elections, Dean Barnes would send a letter congratulating the new student body president. After a paragraph heaping praise on the new leader's skills, the letter would turn to trash. "Is there anything we can do about the litter on this campus?" he would ask.

He loathed litter.

Rarely did I ever see him walking across campus without his hands filled with candy bar wrappers, discarded paper soda cups and other junk he had collected along the miles of sidewalks.

It was quite a sight to see a college administrator, decked out in suit and tie, bending down to scoop up an elusive piece of scrap paper being blown about by the prairie wind. After corralling the rubbish, he would survey the landscape, looking for the nearest trash barrel. He bee-lined to the receptacle, dumped the refuse, and grandly slapped his hands together, seemingly to get rid of unwanted residue. There would be a slight pause, and then he would whirl around and proceed to his destination.

This was leadership by example. He knew college students were watching. I am convinced he wanted people to take notice and change their behavior. He was trying to teach two lessons. First, don't litter. Second, if you see litter, pick it up.

Allen Barnes died in April 1999. But, whenever I see trash while walking on the campus, I think of him. Then, the guilt sets in. So, I smile, pick up the litter and find a trash can.

I remember, Dean Barnes, I remember.

HALL OF FAMER

The first time I shook hands with Jim Langer I couldn't believe the size of his fingers. I don't remember where I met him, but I remember the fingers. Oh, and the thick, black mustache, too.

Langer, a native of Royalton, Minnesota, graduated from SDSU in 1970. He was a darned good baseball player. In 1969 he led the North Central Conference in hits and had a 1.57 earned run average as a pitcher, thus earning All-America honors. In football, Langer played tackle and guard on offense and linebacker on defense. It's ironic he didn't play center – the position that would bring him fame.

Erv Heuther, former SDSU baseball and football coach, told me he convinced a scout for the Cleveland Brown's football team to give Langer a shot at professional football. The Browns eventually released him, but the Miami Dolphins quickly signed him. Two years later, Langer played every down in the Dolphins' 1972 heralded and undefeated season, going 17-0.

In 1987, he was inducted into the Professional Football Hall of Fame, located in Canton, Ohio. He's the only member of the now-defunct North Central Conference ever to achieve this honor. That's remarkable considering the conference stood for eighty-six years.

One year later, Langer was inducted into the Jackrabbit Sports Hall of Fame. Some people might find it odd that he made it into the hallowed halls of Canton before he joined his alma mater's elite group. Under the rules for the Jackrabbit Sports Hall of Fame, established in the '60s, a former SDSU student-athlete wasn't eligible for the coveted honor until twenty-five years after graduation. That meant Langer had to wait until 1995. Rightfully, the rule was waived.

A bust of Jim Langer is in the Ginn Trophy Room, located on the second floor of the Stanley J. Marshall Athletic Complex. It is a duplicate of the bust that proudly rests at the Professional Football Hall of Fame.

Whenever I think of that bust, I remember a Saturday in the early '90s. I was still working in the athletic department. It was a recruiting weekend for the football program. Prospective athletes and their parents showed up and got treated like royalty.

Outside, at old Huether Field, Langer was playing first base for the alumni baseball team. I went to Mike Daly, then head football coach, and asked him if he thought it would be a good idea to have Langer speak to the prospects and their families. He quickly agreed.

So, I walked over to the baseball field and asked Langer if he would like to visit with the assembled group. "Yup, no problem," was his reply.

A half hour later Langer stood in front of his bust in the Ginn Trophy Room. He was wearing a gray sweat suit and on his head was a blue SDSU baseball cap adorned with the blocked SD insignia.

Coach Daly introduced Langer. Then, Langer proceeded to talk about his experience at SDSU. He didn't talk long but his words had an impact. At least they did to me.

I was standing off to his left, facing the young men and their parents. Toward the end of his talk, Jim said, "I played against guys from Notre Dame and Southern Cal. And, do you know what I learned?"

There was absolute silence; nobody even breathed.

All eyes in that room were fixed on Jim's mouth, waiting for his next words. Then Jim said, "I learned I could kick a Wolverine's (Michigan) ass!"

Again, silence.

Every recruit and his family sat with eyes wide open, blank stares on their faces, not knowing how to react. Seeing all this, I burst out laughing.

Jim, in his own unique way, was telling those young men that if they attended SDSU, they too could compete on the national stage. Maybe not in football, but in life. They didn't have to take a backseat to anybody.

Great advice.

Coming of Age

My daughter, Molly, was nine years old when she asked me a question that first made me smile – then think.

It was in 1992 and I was serving as an assistant to the athletic director. Back then, there were numerous basketball doubleheaders, meaning the women's game tipped off at 6 p.m. and the men's game followed at around 8 p.m.

Molly and I arrived a half an hour before the start of the women's contest and sat on the old wood bleachers under the west basket in Frost Arena. As usual, the national anthem kicked in five minutes before the game. There was no pep band so the music came over the loud speakers courtesy of a cassette tape. The public address announcer simply asked the people to rise and the anthem was played. A smattering of applause followed. Fewer than five hundred people don't make a lot of noise in a cavernous arena.

Fast forward to the start of the men's game. By that time, the season ticket holders had finally showed up and the seats were filled. The pep band had arrived, too, and was playing loud, raucous music.

The public address announcer asked the crowd to stand for the playing of the national anthem. Four members of the SDSU ROTC unit, in neatly attired military uniforms, marched in precision fashion onto the floor carrying the American flag. After the pep band played a rousing rendition of the anthem, the color guard retreated.

Upon seeing all this, Molly asked, "Dad, why don't we get soldiers?"

In her young mind, she saw disparity in the form of soldiers – or a lack of them. She could have mentioned the absence of a pep band or far fewer fans, but she picked soldiers.

A lot has changed since then, but in 1992, the women's basketball games weren't even broadcast on the radio. That was still a few years away.

At the time, women's basketball at SDSU was good and getting better. Legendary coach Nancy Neiber was fashioning a program to compete for a North Central Conference title. And, as history has shown, if you won the conference championship, you were poised to take a run at the national crown.

Coach Neiber was a pioneer. As a youngster growing up in Pierre, South Dakota, she had witnessed first-hand the harsh unfairness of girls wanting to play sports. One day she tucked her hair underneath a baseball cap and tried out for a little league team. When her cap fell off, her cover was blown and she was sent away. No girls allowed.

When I attended SDSU in the '70s, women's athletics were a bit of an enigma. Most of us came from high schools where sports weren't offered to girls. Where did those female jocks come from?

As I later learned, especially during my days as alumni director, the road for them wasn't easy. Scholarships were but a dream. There wasn't even enough money for a full complement of uniforms. In the '70s, the women wore the same uniforms for the volleyball, basketball and track seasons.

This caused some tension and anxiety among the athletic staff. In fairness, I believe everyone was trying to do the best they could with what they had. Money was tight and it was difficult to carve out enough dollars from the budget to keep everyone happy. The concept of fundraising was still in its infancy and corporate sponsorships were many years away.

According to Nancy Neiber, "South Dakota State was ahead of the curve," with respect to support of women's athletics.

As a society, we have progressed. Young people, in general, don't have a clue about the struggles of the early years in women's athletics. All they know is what they see – now.

In 1972, Title IX became the law of the land. The statute, in very simple language, states: "No person in the United States shall on the basis of sex, be denied the benefits of, or be subjected to discrimination under any education program or activity receiving Federal financial assistance."

No mention was made of athletics but it has become the public face of the legislation.

It has been heralded and damned. State legislatures to local school boards have wrestled with it. Critics argued that men's programs would suffer because resources would be redirected to the women's programs. Or even, they feared, some male sports would be completely eliminated.

With its genesis in the volatile '70s, long-held ideas on a woman's place in society were being threatened at every level. Demands for equal pay, job access and upward mobility challenged the old order. Now, equal opportunities for women in sports?

The world loved by Archie Bunker-types and their ilk had been shaken. What next – a black president?

On March 29, 2003, I was in St. Joseph, Missouri, when the SDSU women won the national Division II basketball championship. They beat Northern Kentucky, 65-50, for the title.

Nancy Neiber was there, too. Retired from coaching, the veteran warrior deserved to be there to watch what she had helped create. I can't imagine what she felt when the final buzzer sounded.

As members of the team lay on the basketball floor of the St. Joseph Civic Arena, pretending to make snow angels, I struggled with my emotions. I was witnessing young women celebrate an achievement few have known. Or, in my generation, could never have thought possible.

In the joy of the moment, I remembered what my daughter, Molly, had asked me in 1992.

I looked around and saw nearly three thousand fans, dubbed "Jackrabbit Nation" by the local media, standing on their feet, screaming and yelling their approval. The pep band was there, too, having traveled the four hundred miles to support their team.

The world had changed. And, the world changed again on March 10, 2009, when the SDSU women became the first South Dakota team to earn a spot in the NCAA Division I tournament - the Big Dance.

So yes, Molly, now before the start of women's basketball games, you get soldiers, too.

Meeting Royalty

On April 30, 1998, I met a genuine hero. He wasn't a great athlete, a movie star, or for that matter, a famous person. But when I met him, I could not say a word.

His name was Michael Fitzmaurice. Around his neatly pressed white shirt collar was a pale blue ribbon with a gold star dangling from it. It was the Medal of Honor – the nation's highest citation given to a member of the military.

First off, you don't *win* the Medal of Honor. Most of the time, it costs the life of the recipient. Besides, no person ever to attain the distinction went looking for it. In a moment of pure hell, ultimate courage prevailed. It is an award given to the bravest of the brave.

At that moment, I was shaking the hand of royalty and nothing would come out of my mouth. Nothing.

Seeing a real hero will do that to you.

I met Mr. Fitzmaurice on the day South Dakota State University was honoring the memory of Willibald "Bill" Bianchi, a member of the class of 1940. Bianchi is the only SDSU graduate ever to be awarded the Medal of Honor. A native of New Ulm, Minnesota, Bianchi received the news while lying in a U.S. Army hospital bed in the Philippines, recovering from the wounds he had received on February 3, 1942.

A bronze plaque featuring a uniformed Bianchi hangs in a stairwell of the University Student Union and gives the details of that fateful day:

"When the rifle platoon of another company was ordered to wipe out two strong enemy machine gun nests, Lieutenant Bianchi voluntarily and of his initiative, advanced with the platoon leading part of the men. When wounded early in the action by two bullets through the left hand, he did not stop for first aid but discarded his rifle and began firing a pistol. He located a machine gun nest and personally silenced it with grenades. When wounded a second time by two machine-gun bullets through the chest muscles, Lieutenant Bianchi climbed to the top of an American tank, manned its anti-aircraft machine gun, and fired into strongly held enemy positions until knocked completely off the tank by a third severe wound."

Because of Bianchi's brave actions, his platoon lost no men. After a month in the hospital, he was promoted to captain and returned to his unit.

A month later, when American forces surrendered to the Japanese, Bianchi and 75,000 other United States and Filipino soldiers were forced to endure the infamous Baatan Death March. It is estimated that two of every three soldiers alive at the time of the surrender did not live to see the end of the war.

Bianchi was one of those unfortunate souls. For almost three years, Bianchi faced hunger and beatings as a prisoner of war. With defeat imminent, the Japanese moved the POWs onto boats, referred to as "Hell Ships." On January 9, 1945, Bianchi was in the hold of one such ship, the Enoura Maru, when an American plane bombed it. He was killed instantly.

It was a sad ending for a real patriot.

A little more than fifty years after Bianchi's death, Tom Beattie, a retired SDSU faculty member, encouraged the Alumni Association and university to give proper recognition to a genuine hero. Being a WWII veteran himself, Tom was passionate about this.

On April 30, 1998, we did just that. Bianchi family members, Governor Bill Janklow, a contingent of dignitaries from New Ulm, SDSU military personnel and a host of other grateful individuals showed up.

And so did Michael Fitzmaurice.

He was there to pay his respects to a brother in arms, a fellow member of a very elite group. Since 1863, a total of 3,466 Medals of Honor have been awarded. There are fewer than one hundred living recipients, and the number is dwindling rapidly with the passing of the WWII generation.

Allow me a layman's explanation of what Fitzmaurice did on March 23, 1971. The place was Khesanh, South Vietnam.

It was 2 a.m. and intermittent shelling by the North Vietnamese turned into an all-out suicidal mission by the enemy. Fitzmaurice was with three fellow soldiers when suddenly two hand grenades were thrown into their bunker. Without flinching, Fitzmaurice scooped them up and tossed them out of the bunker.

A third grenade came flying in and landed close to Fitzmaurice's feet. With complete disregard for his own safety, he threw his flak jacket and himself over the grenade.

The blast ripped hot shrapnel into his body and blinded his left eye. His unselfish action saved his fellow soldiers.

Figuring the end was near and he wasn't going to die without putting up a good fight, Fitzmaurice grabbed his rifle, jumped out of the trench and started shooting at the advancing North Vietnamese. Another enemy grenade was tossed his way and when it exploded it knocked the rifle out of his hands.

In the dark and having the use of only one eye, Fitzmaurice felt around on the ground to find a weapon. At that point, a North Vietnamese soldier jumped on top of him. Fitzmaurice disabled him in hand-to-hand combat.

He found another rifle, jumped back into the trench and resumed firing at the enemy. Although seriously wounded, Fitzmaurice refused to be evacuated until the fight was over.

Besides the loss of his left eye, both of his eardrums were shattered. He spent the next 13 months in the hospital.

Michael Fitzmaurice and Bill Bianchi put their lives on the line, and in doing so, saved the lives of others. As the Good Book reads, "Greater love has no man than this, to lay down his life for his friends."

During Governor Janklow's remarks, he made a surprise announcement. He said that the veteran's facility in Hot Springs, South Dakota, would be renamed "The Michael J. Fitzmaurice Veterans Home." That brought the crowd to its feet. And, it completely caught off guard both Fitzmaurice and his wife. As the crowd clapped, Fitzmaurice stood stunned, his eyes blinking rapidly, and his wife cried.

It was one of those rare, marvelous moments in life where you felt it was a real privilege to be there.

Tom Beattie was interviewed for the chapter on Bill Bianchi in the book, "The College on the Hill." Beattie said, "We've (he and his wife, Pat) traveled some...and in Europe, every town has a square that has some hero. They don't forget their heroes. We do. That was the big thing with me. That's why I wanted Bianchi's plaque in the Union – so every kid would see what a hero was."

Thanks to Tom's vision, I got to shake the hand of Michael Fitzmaurice. I now know what a real hero looks like.

A Long Way From Home

There are magical moments in life that defy description. Writers fall short finding the right words to adequately describe an event or happening that takes one's breath away. My shortcomings aside, I will do my best to share one of my favorite stories.

In March 2001, I found myself at the Cambridge American Cemetery located just outside Cambridge, England. The grounds serve as the final resting place for 3,812 United States servicemen and women who perished in World War II. It's a beautiful place where people don't talk. Only the chirping of birds and wind rustling through the trees can be heard.

I was there with the SDSU Concert Choir. The great director of the sixty-six-member choir, Dr. Charles Canaan, had asked me to serve as a chaperone. I gladly accepted as three years before that, in 1998, I had joined the choir in making a similar trip. There were some new faces, but the voices were just as beautiful as before.

In our overseas visit in 1998, we stopped at the cemetery. After walking around the immaculately groomed grounds and taking in the enormity of seeing all those perfectly aligned white cross tombstones in a sea of green grass, members of the choir assembled in a small chapel. Then, in a spontaneous moment, fueled by their newfound patriotism, they sang the national anthem.

When they were done singing, there was absolute silence. No one spoke for five minutes. Tears could be seen running down the faces of many choir members.

All of it was wonderful and so right.

A few weeks later, after we returned to Brookings, a reporter for *The Brookings Register* contacted Mike Ehlers, a member of the choir. Mike, a Huron, South Dakota, native, was asked about his favorite moment from the trip. Mind you, we visited marvelous places and the choir sang in huge cathedrals that were more than eight hundred years old. Some members of the choir had a brief encounter with Mick Jagger, lead singer of the Rolling Stones, at a Hard Rock Café. Yet, Mike told the reporter that his fondest memory was singing the national anthem in the cemetery.

I could have kissed him.

People contacted us after reading the newspaper and we discovered that three men buried in the cemetery had connections to Brookings or SDSU. Armed with this new information, we were determined to honor those individuals when we returned in March 2001.

Before making the trip, we ordered flowers to decorate the graves of George Bell, Carol Larson and Robert McCormick.

Bell was the brother of Dr. Rodney Bell, longtime head of the SDSU history department. Dr. Bell and his wife, Fayne, were at the cemetery when we arrived. He had retired from the university a few years earlier. It was his first trip to that hallowed place.

The choir gathered around George Bell's grave. Dr. Bell, in a voice barely above a whisper, said his brother had died on Christmas Eve 1943. It devastated his mother so much that the joy of the Christmas season, for her, was never the same. She never got over the loss.

After he spoke, the choir sang the moving and comforting Christian hymn, "Abide With Me."

At the gravesite of Carol Larson, I shared the story that was relayed to me by his brother, Lorys, a retired faculty member at SDSU. A Brookings native and decorated Army pilot, Larson had flown fifty bombing missions in the Euopean Theater of Operations. On his last mission, he was returning to his British airbase, but was ordered to stay aloft until aircraft carrying casualties landed first. Not able to gain landing clearance, his plane eventually ran out of fuel, and he crashed into a grove of trees. Carol Larson was only twenty-six years old.

Once again, the choir sang "Abide With Me."

The third gravesite belonged to Robert McCormick. I wanted the students to know that he was a fellow Jackrabbit, class of 1939. He had been an engineering major from Sioux Falls and vice president of the student body. Then I told them a story shared with me by McCormick's college classmate, Palmer Dragston, just before we made the trip to England.

Dragston said that on a summer day in 1943, he and a few members of his Army unit were walking down a road just outside of London, England. A convoy of U.S. Army trucks drove past and came to a grinding halt. A soldier jumped out and yelled, "Hey, Pinky!"

"Pinky" was Dragston's college nickname. The soldier who shouted it out was Capt. Robert McCormick.

Dragston told me that McCormick recognized him by the way he walked as he had seen him do so many times on State's campus.

They soon got together and went boating on the famous River Thames. It was a beautiful day, Dragston said, as they reminisced about old times back in South Dakota. When the day was done, the two agreed to meet again.

It was a meeting that would never take place. On October 9, 1943, McCormick attempted to disarm a live bomb that was discovered on the English coastline. The weapon detonated prematurely, taking the life of Capt. McCormick. He left a wife and young son.

I wanted the choir members to know they had a personal connection to the man who was now buried thousands of miles from home. Though separated by two generations and an ocean, they were banded together by a common place – their university. He had walked where they now walk.

After I was done speaking, the choir huddled around McCormick's grave and sang "The Yellow and Blue," our alma mater song.

The emotions poured out of them – young people from small towns like Gettysburg, Miller and Armour, places Robert McCormick was familiar with when he was a student. And now, those young people from the faraway South Dakota prairie were honoring him by singing the same words he had sung as a young man sixty years before.

We come from the Sioux and the Missouri
The Cheyenne and the Jim

*From the pine clad peaks of the Black Hills
Brimful of vigor and vim;
We sing the song of the prairie
The home of the Yellow and Blue
The gleaming gold of the cornfields
The flax of azure hue.*

*Oh SDSU
Hurrah for the Yellow and Blue
Old SDSU
All glory and honor to you
Forever raise the song
In praise both loud and long
With loyal hearts so true...so true.*

It is a moment I will remember for the rest of my life.

Author reading Capt. McCormick's story.

Inspiring...heartwarming...
         makes you count your blessings.

A true story about how one man
made a big difference.

Get your autographed copy by going to:
www.lifesgreatmoments.com